VATC

The Collected Writings

DRE

of Renzo Novatore

translated by

Wolfi Landstreicher

UNION OF EGOISTS
STAND ALONE

NOVATORE
The Collected Writings of Renzo Novatore
By Renzo Novatore
Introduction by Wolfi Landstreicher
Translated by Wolfi Landstreicher
Typeset and Designed by Kevin I. Slaughter

The first edition of *The Collected Writings of Renzo Novatore* was published by Little Black Cart in 2012. In 2023, publisher and distributor Little Black Cart ceased perations.

This newly typeset edition has been issued by the Union of Egoists in 2025 throught its Stand Alone project.
It retains all the material from the first edition.

More information:
UnionOfEgoists.com
UnderworldAmusements.com

Introduction

In reading through and translating the writings of Renzo Novatore (a task that never felt like work, but always like intense and passionate play), I found not only a poetic rebelliousness, but also the sort of coherence an egoist perspective can bring to the way an individual confronts life.

By the time he was eighteen, he considered himself an anarchist and his practical conflict with the social order was immediately evident in attacks on what society declared sacred. But the earliest writings I was able to find are from 1917, when he was about twenty-seven. Here his egoist and individualist perspective is already evident in his focus on immediate rebellion in the here and now, in his hatred for the variations on the social herd mentality in practice—democracy, socialism, fascism—and in his contempt for those willing slaves, the "bourgeois toads" and the "proletarian frogs." The way most responded to government orders to go to the slaughter of World War I deserved nothing but such contempt. At the same time, the early writings also reflect the influence that anarchist-communist ideas had on the youthful Novatore. In *Toward the Creative Nothing*, Novatore expresses his hope for a revolution that will "communalize material wealth" as it will "individualize spiritual wealth." And in this epic expression of poetic rebellion, as well as in the much briefer "Toward the Conquest of New Dawns," Novatore imagines the coming of a new dawn of freedom that will then lead to the Great Noon. Here the influences of Oscar Wilde and Nietzsche on Novatore are evident. In *The Soul of Man Under Socialism*, Wilde calls for a form of anarchist-communism on the material level, precisely so that individuals could fully live out their uniqueness. And Nietzsche never completely eradicated the idea of a something higher for you and I to achieve... as ambiguous as his "overhuman" (Übermensch) may be, he still seems to refer it to the future, and certainly the Nietzschean "Great Noon" is yet to come. So at this point in Novatore's life perhaps he still has too much faith in a future, and yet this may simply be a response to social ferment that was stirring elsewhere. This was, after all, the year of the Russian revolution.

Through much of 1918 and 1919, Novatore was on the lam, because he had deserted the Italian army after being drafted to fight in World War I and had been sentenced to death. I could find no writings by him from 1918, and he wrote a number of the writings from 1919 under a pseudonym. It seems that in his writings from this time on, Novatore stopped talking of any "communalization of material wealth." Instead, there is "the expropriator," who is "a child of the distant future fallen into the world by chance," and for whom "crime is the highest synthesis of freedom and life." Then in September 1920, when workers all over Italy take over their workplaces in rebellion against their masters, Novatore doesn't speak of any positive vision of the future. The only "hope" he expresses is for the destruction of the current social order and all its values. What he finds worth-while in this movement is that, at least for the time being, the "stupid and deceitful idea that property is something 'sacred and inviolable' has been swept away from the minds of the masses...," but one shouldn't take this to mean that Novatore had any faith in the masses. He explains his support of the 1920 rebellion: "The proletariat bowed and resigned under the burden of enslavement disgusts me.... The proletariat in revolt is quite a pleasure for me. And I enjoy seeing the idiotic bourgeoisie weeping and despairing because the sacred table of the right to property has fallen broken under the rebellious fist of the new force." But he recognizes that such large-scale uprisings are moments, and that sooner or later the "proletariat" will "stop to bow its tired head under the lash of a new master or ... let itself be ruled by the grotesque and obtuse will of its utterly cowardly leaders..." And when they stop? "... my revolution will continue to blaze even when the collective one is extinguished under the spout of the red pumps made available to the yellow bourgeoisie. But blending my fire a bit with that of the universe 'when it is in flames' is a fine caprice for me.

Who isn't aware that individualists of my type are bizarre, capricious and strange?" So says this darkly playful vagabond rebel.

If, in Novatore's earlier writings (and the two or three from the time of the workers' rebellion and workplace occupations of 1920), hope for a world in which all individuals can spend their life in striving for their own realization rather than serving a master is a major factor, nevertheless, even here, what is central is the immediate expression and fulfillment of oneself here and now in destructive rebellion against everything that makes one a slave. This is the coherent egoist thread that runs through all of Novatore's writings presented in this volume. There are times when egoists may take joy in a large scale rebellion, times when they may even participate, but always with the awareness that these rebellions will end, if not defeated, then in the creation of new social arrangements, and in those arrangements, those of us who prefer never to be arranged will continue to rebel, and in our rebellion will mock those who let themselves embrace a new slavery. This was Novatore's coherent egoist path, which he followed till the day he was killed in a shootout with carabinieri at a tavern in Teglio, Italy.

Wolfi Landstreicher

Biographical Note

Renzo Novatore was the penname of Abele Rizieri Ferrari who was born in Arcola, Italy (a village of La Spezia) on May 12, 1890 to a poor peasant family. Unwilling to adapt to scholastic discipline, he only attended a few months of the first grade of grammar school and then left school forever. Though his father forced him to work on the farm, his strong will and thirst for knowledge led him to become a self-taught poet and philosopher. Exploring these matters outside the limits imposed by the educational system, as a youth he read Stirner, Nietzsche, Wilde, Ibsen, Baudelaire, Schopenhauer and many others with a critical mind.

From 1908 on, he considered himself an anarchist. In 1910, he was charged with the burning of a local church and spent three months in prison. A year later, he went on the lam for several months because the police wanted him for theft and robbery. On September 30, 1911, the police arrested him for vandalism. In 1914, he began to write for anarchist papers. He was drafted during the first World War. He deserted his regiment on April 26, 1918 and was sentenced to death by a military tribunal for desertion and high treason on October 31. He left his village and went on the lam, propagating armed uprisings against the state.

On June 30, 1919, a farmer sold him to the police after an uprising in La Spezia. He was sentenced to ten years in prison, but was released in a general amnesty a few months later. He rejoined the anarchist movement and took part in various insurrectionary endeavors. In 1920, the police arrested him again for an armed assault on an arms depository at the naval barracks in Val di Fornola. Several months later, he was free, and participated in another insurrectionary endeavor that failed because of a snitch.

In the summer of 1922, three trucks full of fascists stopped in front of his home, where he lived with his wife and two sons. The fascists surrounded the house, but Novatore used grenades against them and was able to escape. He went underground one more time.

On November 29, 1922, Novatore and his comrade, Sante Pollastro, went into a tavern in Teglia. Three carabinieri (Italian military police) followed them inside. When the two anarchists tried to leave, the carabinieri began shooting. The warrant officer killed Novatore, but was then killed by Pollastro. One carabiniere ran away, and the last begged Pollastro for mercy. The anarchist escaped without shooting him.

Renzo Novatore wrote for many anarchist papers (*Cronaca Libertaria*, *Il Libertario*, *Iconoclasta!*, *Gli Scamiciati*, *Nichilismo*, *Pagine Libere*, etc.) where he debated with other anarchists (among them Camillo Berneri). He published a magazine, *Vertice*, that has unfortunately been lost. In 1924, an individualist anarchist group published two pamphlets of his writings: *Al Disopra dell'Arco* (*Over the Arch*) and *Verso il Nulla Creatore* (*Toward the Creative Nothing*).

CONTENTS

1921

1922

1923

posthumous

1917

Thoughts and Sayings

Man owes his arm to the Republic, his intelligence to the gods, his person to the family; but the feelings of his heart are free. So wrote Plato.

But I don't agree with any of this except what relates to the feeling of the heart; the rest, aside from being very questionable, could also be detestable.

●

Trailus wrote: *I don't want to be myself, or have knowledge of what I feel.* And I note with bitter sadness that there are so many who have carried out this terrifying curse of his, and, what is worse, who want to impose it as the gospel of life on their children.

●

The one who has found himself again hears songs of freedom and victory echoing in the depths of his spirit.

●

If God did not exist, it would be necessary to invent him, Voltaire affirmed; fortunately Bakunin answered: *If god existed, it would be necessary to kill him.*

●

The soul restored to itself, alone in possession of all its being and all its power, naturally catches a glimpse of and feels this something inaccessible to reason. So wrote Thaumassin. But which of you doesn't know that he was a theologian?

●

There is no greater sign of being not much of a philosopher and not much of a wise man than wanting all of life to be wise and philosophical. So Leopardi concluded, and in saying this he spoke a great truth. But today the collective madness has passed the sign by far, and the sad and melancholy poet of Sorrow cannot have any moral responsibility in this sinister event.

●

Tacitus was mercilessly relentless against all those responsible for the atrocious wars that devastated all humanity in his times. But Tacitus lived in one of those unhappy (?) times when wars were called "barbarism" even by great historians like he himself. Meanwhile in our and Benedetto Croce's century, instead war is called "civilization"! When one speaks of the times!

•

Lucretius, who lived in a time saturated with the horrors of war, sang his solemn lyrical compositions to Venus, goddess of Love, begging her to placate the fierce wrath of Mars.

Gabriele D'Annunzio, acting as the new Homer (?), plucks his lyre making his hosanna pour out to the bestial god of war so that he can become still more bestial and cruel.

This may also be a question of the times, but I believe that it is rather a question of vanity and of... cash!

•

Horace, addressing himself—as one would say in modern language—to the "civilizers" of his time, exclaimed: *Are you swept away in a blind rage?—Answer me! They are silent—* He goes on: *A ghastly pallor colors their faces; it is the crime of fratricide going back to the time when the blood of Remus fell on the earth abhorrent to grandchildren.* But Horace had been dead a long time and the "ghastly pallor" no longer colors the face of our warriors.

Il Libertario, La Spezia, vol.XVI, no.695

Cry of Rebellion

Dedicated to the rabble.
The fall of peoples and of humanity
will be the signal of my rising.
—Max Stirner

The restless, questioning spirit of the new human beings can no longer nurture themselves on Socrates' historical hemlock and Christ's legendary cross.

These two sacrifices, which have now fortunately fallen into the deep chasms of a shadowy past, were—undoubtedly—consummated completely at the expense of vigorous individualities, straining and throbbing manifestations of free life.

And I profess that, in contrast to Socrates and Christ, Diogenes himself seems to me to be a truly great innovator, since his wine cask has a different and much deeper meaning than Socrates' hemlock or Christ's cross.

But if Socrates and Christ, with their useless deaths, struck genuine individual potentialities until they bled horribly, wouldn't all revolutions following their path do the same?

Didn't christianity triumph over the nearly enviable pagan society through a revolutionary dynamic?

And all the liberal, constitutional, absolutist or... democratic republics, empires or monarchies, weren't they all born from torrents of blood, undulating over the scorched lands of war and revolution?

But why did the violent and feverish pulse of every revolution ever shatter, always freely, allowing new phantoms to arise again as sovereign rulers?

The answer is certainly not long in coming since no one will find it hard to understand that all revolutions were domesticated in various ways, and revolutionaries—with the exception of the smallest minority, the "madmen"—were always automatons guided by chimerical and fabulous phantoms.

But what value could those phantoms have for me? What use is any of this to me? To me, the Iconoclast, the killer of phantoms, the demolisher of old and new idols?

What use, for example, could the triumph of christianity be to me? To me, the ultimate anti-christian?

And republics and monarchies, and all the other forms of society that rise as "sacred" sovereigns and can only recognize the "christian", the "subject", the "citizen", the "member", etc., in me? Since I don't consider it hard to understand that in every form of society there must be a "system", indeed, this system, the best of the best: Equality!

But every "sacred" system and all that is Sacred, whether divinely or humanly, demand renunciation and humiliation from me, the Individual. But that's not all.

Because every form of society, born from the fragments of the old one that fell resoundingly into the void, has the conviction that it is the only perfect one. And it is precisely this dogma of perfection that drives it to be so utterly reactionary toward the restless Rebel who does not at all intend to bow before the new God: today, for example, if the revolt against the despot of all Russia finds approval and justification in the foul local papers, they wouldn't approve or justify a damned thing if such a revolt were to break in... the snow-white bosom of... liberal and democratic Italy. Quite the opposite.

But let's take another step forward. Let's suppose, for example, that tomorrow a Republic is proclaimed in Italy. In such a case, wouldn't a very large portion of those who pretend to be furiously revolutionary today, themselves be the fiercest reactionary conservatives of tomorrow?

And if some "hothead", some "madman", some "enthusiast" would want to undermine their new edifice, their brand new God once again? But here I think that I might hear certain good—perhaps too good—people exclaim: But then, isn't he an enemy of the Revolution?!—No, no. Oh, good people, listen to me again since I am so revolutionary that I barely even recognize myself! And do you know why I am a revolutionary who can barely be recognized? For a reason so simple that it is great in its simplicity. Here it is: because I am a revolutionary guided only by the vast and uncontrollable impulse of MY expansion of will and potential.

There is no phantom guiding me, but rather there I am, walking. There is no chimerical dream of a perfect society of universal human redemption, but rather there is the absolute need for my potential affirmation before other potentialities.

God, the State, Society, Humanity, etc. have their own cause for themselves. If I don't want to subjugate myself to God's cause, I am a "sinner". If I don't want to submit to the State, Society, Humanity, I am a "wicked man", a "criminal", a "delinquent".

But what is "sin"? What is "crime"?

Here again, I don't think there is any need for a long and complicated digression to analyze all this, since even children must know by now that the most serious sin that you can commit against divinity is to mock it, not obey it, desecrate it, and deny it. In short, desecrating what is divinely and humanly "sacred" is the greatest "sin", the greatest "crime".

"Sacred"! This is the most monstrous and terrible phantom before which all have trembled up to now.

Here is the old, harsh tablet that the new human beings must shatter!

The FREE SPIRITS, the ICONOCLASTS, all those who have finally discovered in "sin" and "crime" the new spring from which the highest synthesis of life gushes.

And even the rabble, when it learns to quench its thirst at this new, unknown spring, will very quickly realize that it too is a granite potentiality.

But to do this, the rabble will have to stop letting itself be ruled by fear.

Oh, rabble, listen to me! I am not the new Christ come to sacrifice myself on the altar of your redemption. If I did this, I would be a madman and you would be a beggar.

I put my lips to your profane ear and launch a cry. A frightening cry that will make you grow pale. The cry that I launch is that of the great German rebel, Max Stirner. So listen to it, since only by virtue of this magic cry will you vanish as rabble in order to rise up again in the flowering potential of all of your individualized members. Here is the magic cry: *The egoist has always affirmed himself with crime and, with sacrilegious hand, has pulled the sacred idols down from their pedestals. It is necessary to put an end to the sacred; or better still: the need to violate the sacred must become general. It is not a new revolution that approaches; but a mighty, impetuous, superb, shameless, conscienceless crime sounds in the thunder on the horizon. Don't you see how already the foreboding sky grows dark and silent?*

But here again, oh rabble, I see you back away and shout at me with horror: "Whatever is this crime? What does he mean by all this?"

Ah, rabble, rabble! Do you still not understand his speech?

Well, then, listen again. He's the one who's speaking: "Put your hand on whatever you need. Take it; it is yours. This is the declaration of the war of all against all. I alone am the judge of what I want to have." Now do you understand, oh rabble, what is the crime that SOUNDS IN THE THUNDER ON THE HORIZON? But you, oh rabble, may not yet know how to adapt yourself to the idea of eternal war, you who have cradled yourself like a poor baby in the sweet dreams of eternal peace. And who even knows how many idols you still have to worship and on whose altars you still have to sacrifice yourself!

Poor rabble!

And to think that even the blind would have to notice by now that anyone who isn't able to accept eternal war as his affirmation and triumph must accept eternal slavery for the triumph of fabulous phantoms, declared enemies of the *I*.

Yes, oh rabble, I have decided, yet again, to be completely sincere with you. And this is what my sincerity tells you—Today, you sacrifice yourself in blood-soaked trenches for a cause that is not your own. Tomorrow you may sacrifice yourself in lands made bloody by Revolution in order to later allow a new parasitic and corroding worm to rise on the seas of blood that streamed out in hot steaming spurts from your bronze veins so that a new idol could be raised up to sit over you just like the old God.

The consecrated chorus of Love, Pity and social Right will return, making itself heard, skillfully played on new harps, components of the most ancient symphony.

Rabble, listen to me! I still have something more to tell you. What I still have to tell you may well be the thing that weighs on me the most.

So here I am. I am UNIQUE and as long as you remain rabble, I will not be able to associate with you. When I do so, it will be in order to draw you out against my enemy who is your master. But as rabble, you will not allow yourself to be drawn out since you still adore your Lord too much.

You still want to go on living on your knees. But I have understood life.

And anyone who understands life cannot live on his knees.

I have even understood all the traps that the owners of all this have set for me.

When they saw me march boldly to the conquest of my life, armed with all my uninhibited potentiality, they placed before my eager eyes all of their ridiculous and insane phantoms.

They tried to terrorize me with the hobgoblins of the "sacred", but since I, the Iconoclast, the Impious one, scorn and mock all that is "sacred" and "consecrated", and since, like Armida, I destroy the palace in which once I had to suffer enchantment, they threw off their sacred mask and launched themselves against me, imposing the most extreme against me.

That was the day, oh rabble, that I had the true revelation of what life is and what place my *Uniqueness* would have in this.

Now I live on my feet. My eye no longer knows sleep.

I recognize no one's rights against me. Only force can defeat me now, not phantoms.

I said, only force can defeat me. But I also use it. I no longer ask anyone for anything.

I am no beggar.

I only appropriate everything that I have empowered myself to appropriate through the capacity of my potentiality.

My revolution already started a long time ago.

From the moment I knew life, I took up MY weapons and declared MY war.

I struggle for a cause that is my own. No other cause can interest me anymore.

My enemies also struggle for a cause that is *their own* and against me.

But I don't hate them for this.

The REAL interests that they have in fighting against me exempts them from my hatred since I have taken up my weapons against them only due to my REAL interests.

I may very well kill them for my triumph, but without hating them, without despising them; I am not struggling for phantoms!

Rather I despise beggars, misers, all those who don't dare to fight, but who only know how to beg and weep.

They are the ones who beg for fallen crumbs from the sumptuous table of my enemy.

And with these misers of body and spirit my enemy creates a blind and formidable power to launch against me in the battle that has started between we *Egoists*.

But what could these misers ever gain from the victory over me brought back by my enemy, ie, by their master?

Nothing more that the usual crumbs and eternal slavery!

But what are you then, oh rabble, if not the blind, unconscious, begging mass that launches yourself against me in defense of your Lord? Listen to me, oh rabble, you must vanish *as such*, you must have no place in the theater of new life. Do you sneer? Are you maybe lashing out at me?

Could it be that with the blows of my lash I have succeeded in awakening an inner residue of pride in you that slept hidden in the remote corners of your mind that has been servile for centuries?

Already in the distance you can hear the war trumpet sound, announcing the invincible attacks of the Unique ones against the phantoms: the State, Society, God, Humanity...

You turn pale and flee, dragging all your satellites into the abyss of the eternal void; and the rebellious phalange of Free Spirits and Iconoclasts advances into the stormy sky of the Future!

Cronaca Libertaria, vol.1, no.2, August 10

Intellectual Vagabonds

All who appear suspicious, hostile and dangerous to the good bourgeois, Stirner said, *could be brought together under the name "vagabond"; every vagabond way of life displeases the bourgeoisie. And there are also intellectual vagabonds, to whom the hereditary dwelling place of their fathers seems too cramped and oppressive for them to be content any more with its restricted space and so go to find more space and light far away. Instead of remaining curled up in the family cave stirring the ashes of moderate opinion, instead of accepting what has given comfort and relief to thousands of generations as irrefutable truth, they go beyond all the boundaries of tradition and run wild with their impudent criticism and untamed mania for doubt. These extravagant vagabonds form the class of the unstable, the restless, the volatile, formed from the proletariat; and when left to give voice to their unsettled natures, they are called unruly, hot heads, fanatics...*[1]

Oh, intellectual vagabonds! Pale, unrepentant subverters! The ones who gallop on and on through the endless regions of their capricious imaginations that create new things.

While speaking to them, Zarathustra once said: *The earth is still free for great spirits. There are still many harbors for solitary spirits and their kindred, around whom the aroma of tranquil seas drifts. Life is still free, free for the free spirit.*

Then he continued: *Only where the state ceases to exist does the man who is not futile begin: that is where the hymn to the necessary begins, the refrain that is not uniform. There, where the state ceases to exist... but watch a bit, my brothers: don't you see the rainbow over there and the bridges to the overhuman?*

But before telling them all of this, he spoke of the apes and lunatics who bow at the feet of the "new idol"—the state. He said,

---

1   Novatore is not quoting Stirner precisely here, but rather, in part, poetically paraphrasing him.

Oh my brothers, do you want to be suffocated by the breath from their putrid mouths and their unhealthy longings? Instead, shatter the windows and save yourselves in the pure air!

And they—the intellectual vagabonds—shattered the windows and rushed eagerly through the desecrating freedom of the fields, where festive nature wove songs of life; there where the golden crops danced in the wind, kissed by the sun.

From that day forward, they—the subverters—declared themselves outlaws... Enthralled by the seductive charm of freedom won, they almost stayed lying on the ground, resting, when the symbolic murmur coming from the verdant fronds of the mountain called them again, farther... higher... They looked into each other's eyes. The fire of love flashed in each of their pupils like volcanic lava.

They then understood what the Teacher had told them and, recognizing each other as "kindred spirits," they all went off toward the peak of the green mountain that was supposed to reveal new life to them.

When their profaning and sacrilegious feet rested on the high summits, the sun was already setting, leaving nothing of itself but vast red bands that resembled magnificent tongues of fire. At that moment, a sad vision passed through all of their minds. They all seemed to see the Teacher's shadow sinking in those red flames. But in that primitive and desolate silence, they still seemed to hear his voice telling them: "Have no fear. I will rise again with the sun. And now the sunset is ready for you as well, but you too will rise again with the first rays of dawn."

But, alas, turning back to look at each other, they felt a shudder of terror enshrouding them in a mantle of desolation, since the fire of love no longer flowed like volcanic lava in their pupils. The black wings of melancholy beat violently at the door of their hearts filling them with sadness and sleep.

When the dawn came, with its silvery motes, to find the eyes of the free sleepers, to announce the birth of a new day, they leapt to their feet with an even more fiery flame in their eyes. They sang a hymn to life and focused intensely on the distance.

A few moments passed, and then a howl of dionysian joy poured out from all their throbbing breasts.

The rainbow and the bridge to the overhuman, of which the Teacher had spoken, now rose up majestically, brilliantly from the midst of the murky flames of the christian fog.

Gradually, as the sun lit up the horizon, they came to the realization that those regions were already inhabited by other Creatures. Oh, they even recognized these inhabitants... They saw, in all their tragic beauty, Henrik Ibsen's creatures, who with the volcanic fire of passion their eyes, terribly destroyed the gangrenous plagues aimed against the I by social prejudice. And through all that, this symbolic Ibsenian destruction, it seemed to them that they caught sight of the birth of the overhuman.

With silent minds and hearts on fire, they watch Rubek and Irene rise up from the grave to head to where the white flood was waiting, which, saturated with death, sprouted the eternal light of life. But still they watched. They watched and saw! They saw the "Fisherman"—who lived in the "House of Pomegranates" built by Oscar Wilde in the middle of the misty light that emanated from the rainbow rising on the flanks of the overhuman—come out, with his great, irrefutable passion locked in his heart. He launched himself at the priest's house, the Market square, the rock where a young and incredible Mayulda lives and on to the mountain saturated with baleful devices, where she urged him so that she could seduce him in a diabolical witches' dance presided over by the One who could do everything before the appearance of the Fisherman.

But the FISHERMAN challenged everyone, defeated everyone, so impelling is the mad and tenacious desire of his passion. He had to free himself from his soul, the sole obstacle now between him and his heart, since only after this liberation would he be able to freely plunge into the frightening whirlpools of the sea to join his mermaid who lived in the abyss, and who alone could give him the joyous intoxication of love.

Oh, how many things these Intellectual Vagabonds would have seen gleaming between the "rainbow" and the bridges to the overhuman if the uncouth and bestial howl of the vulgar herd—which still vegetates in stagnant waters and grows old without ever renewing itself at the foot of the rocky mountain—had not shaken them, calling them maniacs and lunatics.

A smile of scorn and bitter irony still curled their lips when a red automobile drove ominously through one of the biggest modern cities and, terrible as lightning, propagated a new form of life.

But now I realize that I have wandered. And, worse, in wandering, I have placed myself in bad company... Stirner and Nietzsche, Henrik Ibsen and Oscar Wilde. Is there even a gray automobile? Madmen, degenerates, delinquents, all of them.

Oh, luminaries, you save me from the wrath of decent people... And save me yet again from those who don't take the time to destroy, each day in battle, a bit of this society that oppresses and crushes us, but rather waste their time trying to teach, to impose systems of struggle and thought on those who have tried to learn to struggle and think for themselves. And when their time is not used up in accomplishing all this, it is employed in figuring out how big the lunatic asylums, in which the new rebels against the future society will get locked up, will have to be.

For my part, I find myself in good company with these madmen, and along with one of them—perhaps the best—I cry: "scorn them, scorn the good and the just, since they have always been the beginning of the end." Oh, how well I have lived in the company of these madmen! How great I find their "madness of destruction"! I assure you that I love destructive madness more, far, far more than conserving wisdom.

Yes, yes, leave me with my madmen since I promise you that if the next European revolution denies us the joy of falling wrapped in the delirium of DESTRUCTION, in better times, I will come back to speak of Them, and if there is anything to reproach—perhaps the smallness of their madness?—I will do it and without reserve.

Cronaca libertaria, Milano

Toward the Conquest of New Dawns

On the tree of the future, we build our nest;
eagles bring us food in their hooked beaks.
In truth, a meal that only we, the impure, could enjoy.
They would believe they were eating fire
and would burn their mouths.
—Nietzsche

When the golden fingers of the Sunrise advance over the glazed horizon, intertwined with the silvery fingers of the Dawn, to remove from the new day's pearly face the dark and gloomy veil of the night, I tremble!

I tremble awaiting the Noon!

The noon hour makes the thundering march of Dionysian music echo in my soul!

"Oh, noon hour, noon hour, hurry! Let me see men of light dancing at your side! I still see myself in these friends of mine!"

This is the only prayer that I recite to the morning.

But alas! When the noon hour is passed and the twilight hour approaches, I feel my soul invaded by sadness.

Oh, the terrible vesper hour... When the sun turns to sunset and the day dies... The hour when the last rays of light tenaciously try to resist the implacable invasion of the shadows!

Do you recall? It's been several years, long as centuries, since we were overwhelmed by the twilight shadows of an age that runs toward the sunset, and today we are still in total darkness!

Oh, how I hate the night! How I hate this enemy of sun and light!

This infamous witch of bats and owls!

Oh, Sunrise, new Sunrise, hurry!

Bring us the warm and vibrant long noons of eternity, closed within your golden ivory fingers!

•

But no, it isn't possible to wait for you!

It is necessary to tear open the belly of the night, there is no choice but to secretly abduct you!

We will launch our rousing stone on the roofs of the sleeping city!

We loners...

Oh, yes! Even those who are peacefully wrapped in Morpheus' mantle we will awaken!

They will have to learn to follow us, a small handful of the bold, who jumped to our feet with our destiny in our hands, and, disdainful of those who lethargic sleep has already delivered to death, triumphantly march toward the sublime peaks where the lightning bolts of our spiritual tragedy and our material epic strike!

The moon worshipers and the night's weakened lovers still remain in the swamps: we want light! We will climb onto the bronze rocks of the horizon with the soul full of a solemn and magnificent tragedy, resting in the company of the Dawns! They will solve for us the riddle of the eternal "Why" and explain to us the songs that the winds sing up there!

The strong winds, rising from the virgin forest of the Ideal!

Of the Ideal that watches over the eternal reasons of the Infinite!

"Here is the coming dawn! Here comes my song!" The future calls to us!

And we want to dance over the peaks of the highest mountains kissed by the sun and uncontaminated by the vulgar herd, up there where everything is anarchism and not christianity.

Oh, dawn, oh, dawn! Come lie with us, and we will bring you all the boldness of our virgin forces! We champions of the dream.

We who want to live in the blue sky, because our soul desires this!

We want to destroy everything that is not pure, because our will desires this!

We want to be the eternal advance guard, because our strength desires this!

But we still want to come back in the middle of the night, to place on the leaden roofs of the sleeping city the treasures we've mysteriously stolen, our heart desires this!

And we ask no recompense from the sleepers for all this, for we are born only to give gifts!

The joy of being able to make a gift of our treasures would already be too much for us!

Who, among us, doesn't understand how hard the art of giving gifts is?

But with all this we will give ourselves as a gift! Our egoism, which is to say our love for what men and, yes, also women would have to be, desires this!

And you who listen to us try at least to understand that we are not priests of demagoguery; the nobility of our hearts is too much to let us fall into the shameful devotion to this repulsive craft.

Don't throw that mud on those who know how to leap onto the decks of Freedom and ride rainbows of light, if you don't want to hear them respond with Nietzsche's bitter and violent sarcasm: "Take care not to spit into the wind!"

Show respect to the spirits that desire to decisively break free of everything that is the monstrous birth of the past and the re-sounds: present-day reality.

Respect those who live in the Future!

Our gaze is intensely focused on the gates of the blessed Isle that rises beyond good and evil. That is where the wild, green flowers of our most beautiful hope begin to bloom!

And there, toward that Isle, is where the golden bow of our ship eagerly turns!

Il Libertari, vol.XV, La Spazia, March 17

Wild Flowers

Even throughout the endless, barren lands of the bleak deserts flowers bloom. Flowers that put out a sinful perfume and that make the very hands of those who pick them bleed, but that still have their own splendid history of joy, sorrow, and love. I repeat, they are strange, wild flowers that arise from the nothing that creates. They were fertilized by the sun and then cruelly battered by the storm, thus!

These flowers are thoughts that sprouted in the deep and meditative solitude of my mind, while outside in the world that is no longer mine, madness rages furiously, lashed by the electrifying fire of lightning that strikes relentlessly.

And I, an unrepentant vagabond who loves to run wild on the joyous and frightening paths of this my solitary and deserted realm, will take my pleasure by periodically gathering a bunch of these wild flowers to crown this rebel banner. It was once already brutally crushed in a cowardly way, but it still sings the joyful chorus of eternal return.

•

Only those who have found themselves again after a long, hard desperate search and placed themselves on the margins of society, contemptuous and proud, denying anyone the right to judge them, are anarchists.

Those who are not able to recognize themselves in the greatness of their actions, they alone being their own judge, may believe that they are anarchists, but they are not.

The strength of will and potentiality (not to be confused with power), the spirit of self-elevation and individualization are the first rungs on a long and endless ladder that those who want to surpass themselves along with everything else climb.

Only those who, with impetuous violence, know how to

appraise the rusty gates enclosing the house of the great lie where the lewd thieves of the I (god, state, society, humanity) have arranged to meet, in order to take their greatest treasure back from clammy, greedy hands adorned with the false gold of love, pity, and civilization, from the baleful predators, can consider themselves lord and master of himself and call themselves anarchists.

●

Along with being the greatest rebel, the anarchist also has the merit of being a King. The King of himself, it is understood!

Those who believe that Christ might be the symbol that man should wave in order to achieve the libertarian synthesis of life would have to be a socialist or christian negator of anarchism.

Despite everything, Socrates was undoubtedly much greater than the brutishness of those among his people who condemned him. Nonetheless, when he accepted the hemlock that they sentenced him to drink, he carried out the sort of act of cowardice and devotion that anarchism mercilessly condemns.

●

When an individual uses any means to escape the insurmountable brutishness of a populace made ferocious and brutal by cannibalistic prejudices and frightening ignorance, or the sadistic corruption of a rotten society which believes it has the right to judge and condemn an individual because he carried out a specific action that the above-mentioned society is never at the level to understand, this is a superbly rebellious and individualistic act that can only find its reason for being and its glorification in anarchism.

●

Alas! Up to now, consciousness itself has been an atavistic and fearsome phantom. And it will only cease to be so when a human being has learned how to make it the image and mirror of his own unique will.

●

The first human being who said: "There is no god," was undoubtedly an athlete of human thought. But the one who limited himself to saying that: "The god of the priest does not exist," cheats through equivocation, leaving if sufficiently clear that he is a shady partisan who is already planning to kill people, perhaps with a new lie.

Remain very suspicious of those who limit themselves to the mere negation of god.

Cronaca Libertaria, vol.1, no.8, Milano, September 20

Toward the Creative Nothing

Our time is a time of decadence. Bourgeois-christian-plebeian civilization arrived at the dead end of its evolution a long time ago.

Democracy has arrived!

But under the false splendor of democratic civilization, higher spiritual values have fallen, shattered.

Willful strength, barbarous individuality, free art, heroism, genius, poetry have been scorned, mocked, slandered.

And not in the name of "I", but of the "collective". Not in the name of "the unique one", but of society.

Thus christianity—condemning the primitive and wild force of virgin instinct—killed the vigorously pagan "concept" of the joy of the earth. Democracy—its offspring— glorified itself by justifying this crime and reveling in its grim and vulgar enormity.

Already we knew it!

Christianity had brutally planted the poisoned blade in the healthy, quivering flesh of all humanity; it had caused a cold wave of darkness with mystically brutal fury to dim the serene and festive exultation of the dionysian spirit of our pagan ancestors.

In one cold evening, winter fatally fell upon a warm summer noon. It was—christianity—that, substituting the phantasm of "god" for the vibrant reality of "I", declared itself the fierce enemy of the joy of living and avenged itself knavishly on earthly life.

With christianity Life was sent to mourn in the frightful abysses of the bitterest renunciations; she was pushed toward the glacier of disavowal and death. And from this glacier of disavowal and death, democracy was born.

Thus democracy—the mother of socialism—is the daughter of christianity.

2

With the triumph of democratic civilization the spiritual mob was glorified. With its fierce anti-individualism—democracy—being incapable of understanding such a thing— trampled all the heroic beauty of the anti-collectivist and creative "I".

The bourgeois toads and the proletarian frogs clasped each other's hands in a common spiritual baseness, piously receiving communion from the lead cup containing the slimy liquor of the very social lies that democracy handed to each of them.

And the songs that bourgeois and proletarian raised at their spiritual communion were a common and noisy "Hurrah!" to the victorious and triumphant Goose.

And while the "Hurrah!"'s burst forth high and frenzied, she—democracy—pressed the plebeian cap on her forehead, proclaiming—grim and savage irony—the equal rights...of Man!

This was when the Eagle, in his prudent awareness, beat his titanic wings more swiftly, soaring—disgusted by the trivial performance—toward the peak of meditation.

Thus, the democratic Goose remained queen of the world and lady of all things, imperial mistress and sovereign.

But since something waiting above her laughed, she—by means of socialism, her only true son—moved to hurl a stone and a word, in the low swampy realm where the toads and frogs croaked, to raise a materialistic fistfight in order to make it pass through a titanic war to superb ideas and to spirituality. And in the marshes, the fistfight happened. It happened in such a plebeian manner as to spray mud so high that it stained the stars.

Thus, everything was contaminated with democracy.

Everything!

Even that which was best here.

Even that which was worst here.

In the reign of democracy, the struggles that were opened

between capital and labor were stunted struggles, impotent ghosts of war, deprived of all content of high spirituality and brave revolutionary greatness, unable to create a different concept of life, stronger and more beautiful.

Bourgeois and proletarian, though clashing over questions of class, of power and of the belly, still always remained united in common hatred against the great vagabonds of the spirit, against the solitaries of the idea. Against all those stricken by thought, against all those transfigured by a higher beauty.

With democratic civilization, Christ has triumphed.

In addition to paradise in heaven, "the poor in spirit" had democracy on earth.

If the triumph has not yet been completed, socialism will complete it. In its theoretical conception, it has already announced itself for a long time. It aims to "level" all human worth.

Listen, oh youthful spirits!

The war against the human individual was begun by

Christ in the name of god, was developed by democracy in the name of society and threatens to complete itself in socialism in the name of humanity.

If we are not able to destroy these three absurd and dangerous phantoms in time, the individual will be inexorably lost.

It is necessary that the revolt of the "I" expands itself, broadens itself, generalizes itself!

We—the forerunners of the time—have already lit the beacons!

We have lit the torches of thought.

We have brandished the ax of action.

And we have smashed.

And we have unhinged.

But our individual "crimes" must be the fatal announcement of a great social storm.

The great and dreadful storm that will smash all the structures of conventional lies, that will unhinge the walls of all hypocrisy, that will reduce the old world to a heap of ruins and smoking rubble!

Because it is from these ruins of god, society, family and humanity that the new human mind could be born flourishing and festive, that new human mind that—on the rubble of all the past—will sing the birth of the liberated man: the free and great "I".

3

Christ was a paradoxical misunderstanding from the gospels. He was a sad and sorrowful phenomenon of decadence, born of pagan fatigue.

The Antichrist is the healthy son of all the bold hatred that Life has bred in the secrecy of its own fecund breast, during the twenty and more centuries of christian order.

Because history returns.

Because eternal return is the law that rules the universe.

It is the destiny of the world!

It is the axis around which life itself turns!

To perpetuate itself.

To run itself back.

To contradict itself.

To pursue itself.

To not die.

Because life is a movement, an action.

That pursues thought.

That yearns for thought.

That loves thought.

And this being walks, runs, bustles around.

Life wants to stir in the kingdom of ideas.

But when the way is impractical, then, thought weeps.

It weeps and despairs...

Then weariness makes it weak, renders it christian.

Then it takes its sister life in hand and seeks to confine her in the realm of death.

But the Antichrist—the spirit of the most mysterious and profound instinct—calls Life back to himself, shouting barbarically to her: Let's begin again!

And Life begins again!

Because it does not want to die.

And if Christ symbolizes the weariness of life, the sunset of thought: the death of the idea!

The Antichrist symbolizes the instinct of life.

He symbolizes the resurrection of thought.

The Antichrist is the symbol of a new dawn.

4

If the dying democratic (bourgeois-christian-plebeian) civilization succeeded in leveling the human mind, denying every high spiritual value that stands out above it, it—fortunately—did not succeed in leveling the differences of class, of privilege, and of caste, which—as we have already said—remained divided only over a question of the belly.

Since—for one class as for the other—the belly remained—it is necessary to confess it and not only to confess it—as the supreme ideal. And socialism understood all this.

It understood it, and since it was a skillful—and at last, perhaps, practically useful—speculator, it cast the poison of its coarse doctrine of equality (equality of lice before the sacred majesty of the sovereign state) into the wells of slavery where innocence blissfully quenched its thirst.

But the poison that socialism spread was not the powerful poison capable of giving heroic virtue to anyone who drank it.

No: it was not the radical poison capable of performing the miracle that elevates the human mind—transfiguring it and freeing it. Rather it was a hybrid blend of "yes" and "no". A livid mixture of "authority" and "faith", of "state" and "the future".

So that, through socialism, the proletarian mob once again felt close to the bourgeois mob and together they turned toward the horizon, faithfully awaiting the Sun of the Future!

And this because, while socialism was not able to transform the shivering hands of the slaves into so many iconoclastic, pitiless and rapacious claws, it was also incapable of transforming the mean avarice of the tyrants into the high and superior virtue of generosity.

With socialism, the corrupt and viscous circle created by christianity and developed by democracy was not broken.

Instead it consolidated itself better.

Socialism remained as a dangerous and impractical bridge between the tyrant and the slave; as a false link of conjunction; as the ambiguity of the "yes" and the "no" from which its absurd underlying principle is mixed.

And, once again, we saw the fatally obscene joke that disgusted us. We saw socialism, proletariat and bourgeoisie together, reenter the orbit of the lowest spiritual poverty to worship democracy. But democracy—being government through the bludgeoning of the people by the people—*for the people* as Oscar Wilde once quipped— it was logical that true free spirits, great vagabonds of the idea, more strongly felt the need to push decisively toward the extreme boundary of their iconoclasm of the solitary in order to prepare the trained phalanxes of human eagles in the silent desert, those who will furiously take part in the tragic celebration of the social dusk in order to overturn democratic civilization between their steel claws, and plunge it into the void of an ancient time that was.

5

When the bourgeoisie had kneeled to the right of socialism in the sacred temple of democracy, they serenely stretched out in the bed of expectation to sleep their absurd sleep of peace. But the proletarians, who had lost their happy innocence by drinking the socialist poison, shouted from the left side, upsetting the tranquil sleep of the idiotic, criminal bourgeoisie.

In the meantime, on the higher mountains of thought, the vagabonds of the idea overcame nausea, announcing that something like the roaring laughter of Zarathustra had sinisterly echoed.

The wind of the spirit, like a hurricane, was supposed to penetrate the human mind and raise it impetuously in the whirlwind of ideas in order to overwhelm all the old values from the darkness of time, raising the life of sublimated instinct again in the sun with new thought.

But, awakening, the bourgeois toads understood that some incomprehensible thing cried out in the heights, threatening their base existence. Yes: they understood that a something was coming from the heights like a rock, a roar, a threat.

They understood that the satanic voices of frenzied forerunners of time announced a furious tempest that, arising from the renewed will of a few solitaries, exploded in the entrails of society to raze it to the ground.

But they have not understood (and will never understand this until they have been crushed) that what passed over the world was the powerful wing of a free life in the beating of which was the death of the "bourgeois man" and of the "proletarian man", because all people could have been "unique" and "universal" at the same time.

And this was the reason why all the bourgeoisie of the world rang their bells, made from false idealistic metal, in mass, calling each other to a great assembly.

The assembly was general...

All the bourgeoisie gathered.

They gathered among the slimy rushes growing from the quagmire of their common lies and there, in the silence of the mud, they decided the extermination of the proletarian frogs, their servants, and their friends.

In the ferocious plot all sides were devotees of Christ and of democracy.

All the former apostles of the frogs attended as well. The war was decided and the prince of the black vipers blessed the fratricidal armies in the name of the god who said, "Do not kill", while the symbolic vicar of death implored his goddess who came to dance on the earth.

Then socialism—as skillful acrobat and practical juggler—took a leap ahead. He jumped on the tight wire of sentimental political speculation, his brow encircled in black, and, aching and weeping more or less this way, said, "I am the true enemy of violence. I am the enemy of war, and also the enemy of revolution. I am the enemy of blood."

And after having spoken again of "peace" and "equality", of "faith" and "martyrdom", of "humanity" and "the future", he intoned a song on the motifs of the "yes" and the "no", bowed his head and wept.

He wept the tears of Judas, which are not even the "I wash my hands of it" of Pilate.

And the frogs departed...

They departed toward the realm of supreme human baseness.

They departed toward the mud of all the trenches.

They departed...

And death came!

It came drunk on blood and danced horribly in the world.

For five long years...

It was then that the great vagabonds of the spirit, taken with a new disgust, rode their free eagles once more to soar dizzily in the solitude of their distant glaciers to laugh and curse.

Even the spirit of Zarathustra—the truest lover of war and the most sincere friend of warriors—must have remained sufficiently disgusted and scornful since somebody heard him exclaim: *For me, you must be those who strain your eyes searching for the enemy—your enemy. And in some of you hatred blazes at first glance. You must look for your own enemy, fight your own war. And this for your own ideas!*

And if your idea succumbs, your rectitude cries in triumph!

But alas! The heroic sermon of the liberating barbarian availed nothing.

The human frogs knew neither how to distinguish their own enemy nor how to fight for their own ideas. (The frogs have no ideas!)

And neither recognizing their enemies nor having their own ideas, they fought for the bellies of their brothers in Christ, for their equals in democracy.

They fought against each other for their enemy.

Abel, revived, died for Cain a second time.

But this time, at his own hand!

Willingly...

Willingly, because he could have rebelled, and he did not do so...

Because he could have said: no!

Or yes!

Because saying: "no" he could have been strong!

Because saying: "yes", he could have shown that he "believed" in the "cause" for which he fought.

But he said neither "yes" nor "no".

He went!

From cowardice!

Like always!

He went...

He went toward death!...

Without knowing why.

Like always.

And death came...

It came to dance in the world for five long years!

And it danced hideously in the muddy trenches of all parts of the world.

It danced with feet of lightning...

It danced and laughed...

It laughed and danced...

For five long years!

Ah! How vulgar death is, dancing without the wings of an idea on its back.

What an idiotic thing to die without knowing why...

We saw it—when it danced—Death.

It was a black Death, without transparency of light.

It was a Death without wings!

How ugly and vulgar it was...

How clumsy its dance.

But still it danced!

And how it mowed—dancing—all the superfluous and all of those of the majority. All those for whom—the great liberator tells us—the state was invented.

But alas! It did not mow these alone...

Death—in order to avenge the state—even mowed down those who are not worthless, those who are essential!...

But those who were not worthless, those who were not of the majority, those who have fallen saying "no!" They will be avenged.

We will avenge them.

We will avenge them because they are our brothers!

We will avenge them because they have fallen with stars in their eyes.

Because dying, they have drunk the sun.

The sun of life, the sun of struggle, the sun of an Idea.

6

What has the war renewed?

Where is the heroic transfiguration of the spirit?

Where have they hung the phosphorescent tables of new

values?

In which temple have the holy amphoras of gold that hold the luminous, blazing hearts of the supreme and creative heroes been laid?

Where is the splendor of the great, new noon?

Frightful rivers of blood washed all the turf and covered all the pathways of the world.

Fearful torrents of tears made their heartbreaking lament echo across the eddies of the entire earth: mountains of human bone and flesh everywhere blanched and rotted in the sun.

But nothing was transformed, nothing evolved.

The bourgeois belly merely belched from satiety and that of the proletarian cried out from too much hunger.

And enough!

With Karl Marx the human mind descended into the intestines.

The roar that passes through the world today is a belly roar.

Our will can transform it into a shout of the mind.

Into a spiritual storm.

Into a cry of free life.

Into a hurricane of lightning.

Our thunderbolt could unhinge the present reality, rip open the door to the unknown mystery of our longed-for dream and show the supreme beauty of the liberated man.

Because we are mad forerunners of the time.

Pyres.

Beacons.

Signals.

The first announcements.

7

The war!

Do you remember it?

45

What has the war created?

Here it is:

The woman sold her body and called the prostitution "free love".

The man, who "dodged" to manufacture bullets and to preach the sublime beauty of the war, called his cowardice "delicate artfulness and heroic cunning".

This one who always lived in unconscious infamy, in cowardice, in humility, in indifference, and in weak renunciation, cursed against small audacities—which he had always detested—because by themselves they did not have the strength to prevent his belly from being torn apart by those weapons that he himself had constructed for a vile morsel of bread.

Because even the beggars of the spirit—those who always remain outside to warm up while the more noble part of humanity enters into the hell of life—these humble and devoted servants of their tyrant, these unconscious slanderers of higher minds, even these, we say, did not want to go. They did not want to die.

They writhed, they wept, they implored, they prayed!

But all this from a low instinct of impotent and bestial self-preservation, deprived of every heroic roar of revolt, and not, instead, from questions of a higher humanity, of refined depth of feeling, of spiritual beauty.

No, no, no!

Nothing of all that!

The belly!

Only the bestial belly.

Bourgeois ideal—proletarian ideal—the belly! But in the meantime death came...

It came to dance in the world without having the wings of an idea on its back!

And it danced... It danced and laughed. For five long years...

And while on the borders wingless death danced drunk on

blood, at home in the sacred apse of the internal front— in the vulgar "gazettes" of lies—the miraculous moral and material evolution of our women was recited and sung along with the spiritual peak that our heroic and glorious foot soldier ascended. The one who died weeping without knowing "why".

How many ferocious lies, how much vulgar cynicism the grim minds of democratic society and of the state vomited in the "gazettes".

Who remembers the war? How the crows croaked... The crows and the owls!

And meanwhile death danced!

It danced without having the wings of an idea on its back!

Of a dangerous idea that bears fruit and that creates.

It danced...

It danced and laughed!

And how it mowed—dancing—the superfluous. All those who were of the majority. Those for whom the state was invented.

But alas! It did not only mow these.

It also mowed those who had the rays of the sun, those who had the stars in their eyes!

8

Where is the epic art, the heroic art, the supreme art that the war promised us?

Where is free life, the triumph of the new dawn, the splendor of noon, the festive glory of the sun?

Where is the redemption from material slavery?

Where is the one who has created the fine and profound poetry that was supposed to germinate painfully in this tragic and fearful abyss of blood and death, in order to tell us the silent and cruel torture felt by the human mind?

Who has said the sweet and good word to us that invokes a

clear morning after a terrible night of hurricane?

Who has said the higher word that makes us as great as our sorrow, pure in beauty and deep in humanity?

Who is, who ever is, the genius who was able to bend himself with love and faithfulness over the open wounds in the living flesh of our life, to receive all the noble tears from them so that the supreme laughter of the redeemer spirit could rend the claws from the starving monsters of our past errors in order to make us rise to the concept of a higher ethic, where, through the luminous principle of human beauty purified in blood and sorrow, we could lift ourselves, strong and majestic—like an arrow taut on the bow of the will—to sing the deepest and gentlest melody of the highest of all our hopes to earthly life!

Where? Where?

I don't see it!

I don't feel it!

I look around me, but I see only vulgar pornography and false cynicism...

At least we could have been given a Homer of art, and a Napoleon of the acts of war.

A man who could have had the strength to destroy an epoch, to create a new history... But nothing!

The war has given us neither great singers nor great rulers. Only lying ghosts and grim parodies.

9

The war has passed, washing history and humanity in tears and blood, but the epoch has remained unchanged.

An epoch of disintegration.

Collectivism is dying and individualism has not yet taken hold.

Nobody knows how to obey, nobody knows how to command.

But given all this, knowing how to live free, this is still at present an abyss.

An abyss that can only be filled up with the corpse of slavery and that of authority.

The war could not fill up this abyss. It could only dig it deeper. But what the war could not do, revolution must do.

The war has rendered humans more beastly and plebeian.

Coarser and uglier.

Revolution must render them better.

It must ennoble them.

10

Already—socially speaking—we have slipped down the fatal slope, and there is no more possibility of turning back.

To attempt it alone would be a crime.

Not a great and noble crime however.

But a vulgar crime. A crime more than useless and vain. A crime against the flesh of our ideas. Because we are not the enemies of blood... We are the enemies of vulgarity!

Now that the age of obligation and slavery is agonizing, we want to close the cycle of theoretical and contemplative thought in order to open the breach to violent action, which is still the will of life and the exultation of expansion.

On the ruins of piety and religion we want to erect the creative hardness of our proud hearts.

We are not the admirers of the "ideal man" of "social rights", but the proclaimers of the "actual individual", enemy of social abstractions.

We fight for the liberation of the individual.

For the conquest of life.

For the triumph of our idea.

For the realization of our dreams.

And if our ideas are dangerous, it is because we are those who love to live dangerously.

And if our dreams are mad, it is because we are mad.

But our madness is supreme wisdom.

But our ideas are the heart of life; but our thoughts are the beacons of humanity.

And what the war has not done, revolution must do.

Because revolution is the fire of our will and a need of our solitary minds; it is an obligation of the libertarian aristocracy.

To create new ethical values.

To create new aesthetic values.

To communalize material wealth.

To individualize spiritual wealth.

Because we—violent cerebralists and passional sentimentalists at the same time—understand and know that revolution is a necessity of the silent sorrow that suffers at the bottom and a need of the free spirits who suffer in the heights.

Because if the sorrow that suffers at the bottom wants to rise with the happy smile of the sun, the free spirits who suffer in the heights no longer want to feel the petty offenses of the shame of vulgar slavery that surrounds them.

The human spirit is divided into three streams:

The stream of slavery, the stream of tyranny, the stream of freedom!

With revolution, the last of these streams needs to burst upon the other two and overwhelm them.

It needs to create spiritual beauty, teach the poor the shame of their poverty, and the rich the shame of their wealth.

All that is called "material property", "private property", "exterior property" needs to become what the sun, the light, the sky, the sea, the stars are for individuals.

And this will happen!

It will happen because we—the iconoclasts—will violate it!

Only ethical and spiritual wealth is invulnerable.

This is the true property of individuals. The rest no!

The rest is vulnerable! And all that is vulnerable will be violated!

It will be done by the unbiased might of the "I".

By the heroic strength of the freed man.

And beyond every law, every tyrannical morality, every society, every conception of false humanity...

We must set our endeavor to transform the revolution that advances into "anarchist crime", in order to push humanity beyond the state, beyond socialism.

Toward Anarchy!

If, with the war, people were not able to sublimate themselves in death, death has purified the blood of the fallen.

And the blood that death purified—and that the soil drank greedily—now cries from underground!

And we solitaries, we are not the singers of the belly, but the listeners to the dead; to the voice of the dead who cry from underground!

To the voice of the "impure" blood that is purified in death.

And the blood of the fallen cries!

Cries from under the ground!

And the cry of this blood calls us also toward the abyss... It needs to be freed from its prison!

Oh, young miners, be ready!

We prepare the torches and paravanes.

It is necessary to till the earth.

It is time! It is time! It is time!

The blood of the dead must be freed from its prison.

It wants to rise from the shadowy depths to hurl itself toward the sky and conquer the stars.

Because the stars are the friends of the dead.

They are the good sisters who have seen them die.

They are the ones who go to their graves every night with feet of light and tell them:

Tomorrow!...

And we—the children of tomorrow—have come today to tell you:

It is time! It is time! It is time!

And we have come at the hour before dawn... In the company of the dawn and the last stars!

And to the dead we have added more dead...

But all those who fall have a golden star shining in their eye!

A golden star that says:

"The cowardice of the remaining brothers is transformed into a creative dream, into avenging heroism.

Because if it were not so, one would not deserve to die!" How sad it must be to die.

Without a hope in one's heart... without a pyre in one's brain; without a dream in one's mind; without a golden star shining in our eye!

•

The blood of the dead—our dead—cries from underground.

Clearly and distinctly, we hear that cry. That cry which intoxicates us with anguish and sorrow.

And we cannot be deaf to that voice, nor do we want to... We.

We do not want to be deaf to it, because life has told us:

Whoever is deaf to the voice of blood is not worthy of me.

Because blood is my wine; and the dead my secret.

Only to those who will listen to the voice of the dead will I unveil the enigma of my great mystery!

And we will respond to this voice:

Because only those who know how to respond to the voice from the abyss can conquer the stars.

I address myself to you, oh my brother!

I address myself to you and tell you:

If you are among those who are kneeling in the half circle, close your eyes in the darkness and leap into the abyss.

Only in this way will you be able to bounce back to the highest peaks and open your great eyes wide in the sun.

Because one cannot be of the eagles if one is not of the divers.

One cannot soar to the peaks when one is incapable of the depths.

In the bottom, sorrow dwells, in the heights anguish.

Over the sunset of all the ages, a unique dawn rises between two different dusks.

In the midst of the virgin light of this unique dawn, the sorrow of the diver that is in us must be united to the anguish of the eagle that also lives in us, to celebrate the tragic and fruitful marriage of perpetual renewal.

The renewal of the personal "I" among the collective tempests and social hurricanes.

Because perennial solitude is only for saints who recognize in god their witness. But we are the atheist offspring of solitude.

We are the solitary demons without witness.

In the bottom, we want to live the reality of sorrow; in the heights, the sorrow of the dream...

In order to live all battles, all defeats, all victories, all dreams, all sorrows, and all hopes intensely and dangerously. And we want to sing in the sun; we want to howl in the winds!

Because our brain is a sparkling pyre where the great fire of thought crackles and burns in mad and joyful torments.

Because the purity of all dawns, the flame of all noons, the melancholy of all sunsets, the silence of all tombs, the hatred of all hearts, the murmur of all forests and the smile of all stars are the mysterious notes composing the secret music of our mind overflowing with vital exuberance.

Because in the depth of our heart we hear a voice speaking of human individuation, a voice so masterful and vigorous that, often times, while listening to it, we feel fear and terror.

Because the voice that speaks is His voice: the winged Demon from our depths.

11

Now, it is proven... Life is sorrow!

But we have learned to love sorrow in order to love life! Because in loving sorrow we have learned to struggle.

And in struggle—in struggle alone—is our joy of living.

To remain suspended halfway is not our task.

The half circle symbolizes the ancient "yes and no".

The impotence of life and death.

It is the circle of socialism, of pity and of faith.

But we are not socialists...

We are anarchists. And individualists, and nihilists, and aristocrats.

Because we come from the mountains.

From close to the stars.

We come from the heights: to laugh and to curse!

We have come to light a forest of pyres upon the earth to illuminate it during the night which precedes the great noon.

And our pyres will be extinguished when the fire of the sun bursts majestically over the sea. And if this day should not come, our pyres will continue to crackle tragically amidst the darkness of the eternal night.

Because we love all that is great.

We are the lovers of every miracle, the promoters of every prodigy, the creators of every wonder!

Yes: we know it!

For you, great things are in good as in evil.

But we live beyond good and evil, because all that is great belongs to beauty.

Even "crime".

Even "perversity".

Even "sorrow".

And we want to be great like our crime!

In order not to slander it.

We want to be great like our perversity!

In order to render it conscious.

We want to be great like our sorrow.

In order to be worthy of it.

Because we come from the heights. From the home of Beauty.

We have come to raise a forest of pyres upon the earth to illuminate it during the night which precedes the great noon.

Until the hour in which the fire of the sun bursts majestically over the sea.

Because we want to celebrate the feast of the great human prodigy.

We want our minds to vibrate in a new dream.

We want this tragic social dusk to give our "I" some calm and thrilling tinder of universal light.

Because we are the nihilists of social phantoms.

Because we hear the voice of the blood that cries from underground.

We prepare the paravanes and the torches, oh young miners.

The abyss awaits us. We leap into it in the end: Toward the creative nothing.

12

Our nihilism is not christian nihilism.

We do not deny life.

No! We are the great iconoclasts of the lie.

And all that is declared "sacred" is a lie.

We are the enemies of the "sacred".

And to you a law is "sacred"; a society "sacred"; a moral "sacred"; an idea "sacred"!

But we—the masters and lovers of pitiless strength and strong-willed beauty, of the ravishing idea—we, the iconoclasts of all that is consecrated—we laugh satanically, with a fine broad and mocking laughter.

We laugh!...

And laughing, we keep the bow of our pagan will to enjoy always stretched toward the full integrity of life.

And we write our truths with laughter.

And we write our passions with blood. And we laugh!...

We laugh the fine healthy and red laughter of hatred.

We laugh the fine blue and fresh laughter of love.

We laugh!

But laughing, we remember, with supreme gravity, to be the legitimate offspring and the worthy heirs of a great libertarian aristocracy that transmitted to us satanic outbursts of mad heroism in the blood, and waves of poetry, of solos, of songs in the flesh!

Our brain is a sparkling pyre, where the crackling fire of thought burns in joyful torments.

Our mind is a solitary oasis, always flowering and cheerful, where a secret music sings the complicated melody of our winged mystery.

And in our brain all the winds of the mountains cry to us;

in our flesh all the tempests of the sea shout to us; all the Nymphs of Evil; our dreams are actual heavens inhabited by thrilling virgin muses.

We are the true demons of Life.

The forerunner of the time.

The first announcements!

Our vital exuberance intoxicates us with strength and with scorn.

It teaches us to despise Death.

Today we have reached the tragic celebration of a great social dusk.

The twilight is red.

The sunset is bloody.

Anxiety flaps its throbbing wings in the wind.

Wings red with blood; wings black with death!

In the shadow Sorrow organized the army of her unknown children.

Beauty is in the garden of Life, and is weaving garlands of flowers to crown the brows of the heroes.

The free spirits have already hurled their thunderbolts across the twilight.

As first announcements of fire: first signals of war!

Our epoch is under the wheels of history.

Democratic civilization turns toward the grave.

Bourgeois and plebeian society is shattered fatally, inexorably!

The fascist phenomenon is the most certain and irrefutable proof of it.

To demonstrate it, we would only need to go back in time and question history.

But there is no need for this!

The present speaks with abundant eloquence!

Fascism is nothing but the convulsive and cruel pang of a plebeian society, emasculated and vulgar, that agonizes tragically, drowned in the quagmire of its flaws and of its own lies.

It—fascism—celebrates its bacchanals with pyres of flame and wicked orgies of blood.

But from the gloomy crackle of its livid fires, it does not sparkle with even a single spark of vigorous, innovative spirituality, whereas the blood that it sheds transforms itself into wine that the forerunners of time silently gather in the red chalices of hatred, addressing it as the heroic beverage in order to commune with all the offspring of social sorrow called to the twilight celebration of the dusk.

Because the great forerunners of time are the brothers and the friends of the offspring of sorrow.

Of sorrow that struggles.

Of sorrow that rises.

Of sorrow that creates.

We will take these unknown brothers by the hand to advance together against all the "no" of denial, and to climb together toward all the "yes" of affirmation; toward a new spiritual dawn; toward new noons of life.

Because we are lovers of danger; the reckless ones in all undertakings, the conquerors of the impossible, the promoters and precursors of all "endeavors"!

Because life is an endeavor!

After the negating celebration of the social dusk, we will celebrate the rite of the "I": the great noon of the complete and actual individual.

So that the night triumphs no more.

So that the darkness surrounds us no more.

So that the majestic fire of the sun perpetuates its feast of light in the sky and in the sea.

14

Fascism is an obstacle much too ephemeral and impotent to hinder the course of human thought that bursts beyond every dam and overflows beyond every boundary, stirring action on its way.

Fascism is impotent because it is brute force.

It is matter without spirit; it is night without dawn.

Fascism is the other face of socialism.

Both of them are bodies without minds.

Socialism is the material force that, acting as the shadow of a dogma, resolves and dissolves in a spiritual "no".

Fascism is a consumptive of the spiritual "no" that aims—wretch—at a material "yes".

Both lack willful quality.

They are the bores of time; the temporizers of the deed!

They are reactionary and conservative.

They are crystallized fossils that the strong-willed dynamism of history will sweep away together.

Because, in the willful field of moral and spiritual values, the two enemies are equal.

And it is well known that when fascism is born, socialism alone is its direct accomplice and responsible father.

Because, if when the nation, if when the state, if when democratic Italy, if when bourgeois society trembled in pain and agony in the knotty and powerful hands of the "proletariat" in revolt, socialism had not basely hindered the tragic deadly hold—losing the lamps of reason in front of its wideopened eyes—certainly fascism would never even have been born, let alone lived.

But the awkward colossus without mind is then allowed to take hold—for fear that the vagabonds of the idea would push the movement of revolt beyond the appointed mark— in a most vulgar game of sullen conservative pity and false human love.

Thus, bourgeois Italy, instead of dying, brought forth... It brought forth fascism!

Because fascism is the stunted and deformed creature born of the impotent love of socialism for the bourgeoisie.

One of them is the father, and the other the mother. But neither wants the responsibility for it.

Perhaps they find it a child much too monstrous.

And this is the reason they call it a "bastard"!

And it gets revenge.

Already wretched enough for being born this way, it rebels against the father and insults the mother... And perhaps it has reason...

But we, we bring all this out for history.

For history and for truth, not for ourselves.

For us fascism is a poisonous mushroom planted quite well in the rotten heart of society, that is enough for us.

16

Only the great vagabonds of the idea can—and must—be the luminous spiritual fulcrum of the tempestuous revolution, which advances in gloom upon the world.

Blood requires blood.

That is ancient history!

It can turn back no more.

To attempt to turn back—as socialism does—would be a useless and vain crime.

We must leap into the abyss.

We must answer the voice of the dead.

Of those dead who have fallen with immense golden stars in their eyes.

It is necessary to cultivate the soil.

To free the blood from underground.

Because it wants to rise to the stars.

It wants to burn its good sisters, luminous and distant, who have seen them die.

The dead, our dead, speak:

"We have died with stars in our eyes.

We have died with rays of the sun in our pupils.

We have died with hearts swollen with dreams.

We have died with the song of the most beautiful hope in our mind.

We have died with the fire of an idea in our brain.

We have died..."

How sad death must be as others died—not our dead— without all this in the brain, in the mind, in the heart, in the eyes, in the pupils!

Oh dead, oh dead! Oh our dead! Oh luminous torches!

Oh burning beacons! Oh crackling pyres! Oh dead... Here it is, we are at twilight.

The tragic celebration of the great social dusk draws near.

Our great mind already opens toward the great subterranean light, oh dead!

Because we too have the stars in our eyes, the sun in our pupils, the dream in our heart, the song of hope in our mind and, in our brain, an idea.

Yes, we too, we too!

Oh dead, oh dead! Oh our dead! Oh torches! Oh beacons! Oh pyres!

We have heard you speak in the solemn silence of our deep nights.

You said:

We wanted to rise into the sky of the free sun...

We wanted to rise into the sky of the free life...

We wanted to rise up there where once the penetrating eyes of the pagan poet gazed:

Where great thoughts arise and stand as inviolable oaks among the people; where beauty descends, invoked by pure poets, and stands serene among the people; where love creates life and breathes joy!

Up above where life exults and expands in full harmony of splendor...

And for this, for this dream we struggled, for this great dream we died...

And our struggle was called crime.

But our "crime" must only be considered as titanic valor, as promethean effort for liberation.

Because we are the enemies of all material domination and all spiritual leveling.

Because, beyond all slavery and every dogma, we saw life dance free and naked.

And our death must teach you the beauty of the heroic life! Oh dead, oh dead! Oh our dead...

We have heard your voice...

We have heard it speak this way in the solemn silence of our deep nights.

Deep, deep, deep!

Because we are sensitives.

Our heart is a torch, our mind is a beacon, our brain is a pyre!...

We are the soul of life!...

We are the ones who wake before dawn to drink the dew from the chalice of flowers.

But the flowers have glowing roots attached in the darkness of the earth.

In that earth which has drunk your blood.

Oh dead! Oh our dead!

This, your blood that cries, that roars, that wants to be freed from its prison to hurl itself toward the sky and conquer the stars!

Those, your remote and luminous sisters who have seen you die.

And we—the vagabonds of the spirit, the solitaries of the idea—want our mind, free and great, to open its wings wide in the sun.

We want to celebrate the social dusk in this twilight of bourgeois society so that the final black night is made vermillion with blood.

Because the children of the dawn must be born of blood...

Because the monsters of the darkness must be killed by the dawn...

Because singular new ideas must be born through social tragedies...

Because new people must be forged in the fire!

And only from tragedy, from fire and from blood will the true, profound Antichrist of humanity and of thought be born.

The true child of the earth and the sun.

The Antichrist must be born of the smoking ruins of revolution to enliven the children of the new dawn.

Because the Antichrist is the one who comes from the abyss to rise beyond every boundary.

He is the strong-willed enemy of crystallization, of preestablishment, of conservation!...

He is the one who will drive the human race through the mysterious cavern of the unknown to the perennial unveiling of new sources of life and of thought.

And we—the free spirits, the atheists of solitude, the demons of the desert without witness—have already pushed ourselves toward the most extreme peaks.

Because—with us—everything must be pushed to its maximum consequences.

Even Hatred.

Even violence.

Even crime!

Because Hatred gives strength.

Violence unhinges.

Crime renews.

Cruelty creates.

And we want to unhinge, to renew, to create!

Because everything that is stunted vulgarity must be overcome.

Because all that lives must be great.

Because all that is great belongs to beauty!

And life must be beautiful!

17

We have killed "duty" so that our ardent desire for free brotherhood acquires heroic valor in life.

We have killed "pity" because we are barbarians capable of great love.

We have killed "altruism" because we are generous egoists.

We have killed "philanthropic solidarity" so that the social man unearths his most secret "I" and finds the strength of the "Unique".

Because we know it. Life is tired of having stunted lovers.

Because the earth is tired of feeling itself trampled by long phalanxes of dwarfs chanting christian prayers.

And finally, because we are tired of our brothers, carcasses incapable of peace and war. Too small for hatred and love.

We are tired and disgusted.

Yes, quite tired: quite disgusted! And then that voice of the dead... Of our dead!

The voice of the blood that cries from underground!

Of the blood that wants to free itself from its prison to hurl itself toward the sky and conquer the stars!

Those stars that—blessing them—sparkled in their pupils in the final moment of death, transforming their dreamy eyes into vast discs of gold.

Because the eyes of the dead—of our dead—are discs of gold.

They are luminous meteors that wander the infinite to show us the way.

The way without end that is the pathway to eternity.

The eyes of our dead tell us the "why" of life, showing us the secret fire that burns in our mystery. In that our secret mystery that nobody has sung up to now...

But today the twilight is red...

The sunset is covered with blood...

We are close to the tragic celebration of the great social dusk.

Already, on the bells of history, time has struck the first pre-dawn strokes of a new day.

Enough, enough, enough!

It is the hour of the social tragedy!

We will destroy laughing.

We will set fires laughing.

We will kill laughing.

We will expropriate laughing.

And society will fall.

The fatherland will fall.

The family will fall.

All will fall after the free man is born.

After the one who has learned the Dionysian art of joy and laughter through tears and sorrow is born. The hour has come to drown the enemy in blood... The hour has come to wash our minds in blood.

Enough, enough, enough!

As the poet transforms his lyre into a dagger!

As the philosopher transforms his probe into a bomb!

As the fisherman transforms his oar into a formidable ax.

As the miner comes up from the unbearable caves of the dark mines armed with his shining iron.

As the farmer transforms his fruitful spade into a war lance.

As the laborer transforms his hammer into a scythe and cleaver.

And forward, forward, forward.

It is time, it is time—it is time!

And society will fall.

The fatherland will fall.

The family will fall.

All will fall after the Free Man is born.

Forward, forward, forward, oh joyful destroyers.

Beneath the black edge of death we will conquer Life!

Laughing!

And we will make it our slave!

Laughing!

And we will love it laughing!

Since the only serious people are those who know how to be actively engaged laughing.

And our hatred laughs...

Red laughter. Forward!

Forward, for the destruction of the lie and of the phantoms!

Forward, for the complete conquest of individuality and of Life!

Twilight Ballad

A Symphonic Prelude of "Dynamite"
(*Date of composition unknown.*)

This is the hour of my bleak thoughts.
My Demon sleeps.
The red Demon
of my hellish mirth
sleeps in the gloomy twilight
of this mind of mine.
I smoke...
Desperately, intensely,
I smoke. Always!
Always! Always! Always!
I would like to think, to write, to sing...
But my Demon sleeps
The red Demon
of my hellish mirth
sleeps in the gloomy twilight
of this mind of mine.
And no thoughts come...
Nor even laughter and curses!
This is the dark hour
of my black melancholy.
Distracted, I watch my cigarette,
slender, pale and hot
like an ailing lover.
I watch it consume itself so very slowly
like my life and my dreams
like the lives and dreams of all my brothers.
The ash falls to the ground and is dispersed. So!
The smoke floats off, dense and gray, into the air

and is dispersed as well. So.
There is nothing left for me
but a bit of yellow nicotine on my bitter lip. So.

My Demon sleeps.
The red Demon
of my hellish mirth
sleeps in the gloomy twilight
of this mind of mine.
I look at the sun!
I see it setting among the blond whirlpools
of a golden sea.
Golden and bloody...
But my heart is bitten.
Bitten by a cold sob
without hope or tears,
without hatred or love.
Oh, if only I could weep...
if only I could curse...
But no!
No! No! No!
Who?
Who has ever caused me so much harm?
Who is the malign architect of this suffering of mine?
Alas, mother... my mother...
If I still had the strength
so that at least I could curse you...
But no!
No! No! No!
And yet you—you alone!—
are the one who gave me life,
who gave me sorrow,
who brought me Harm!

But tell me:
Didn't you believe in the joy of living?
Am I, therefore, the child of a grotesque dream?
Or am I rather the lowliest child
of common unawareness?
But then, why, oh mother,
—on that day—
   didn't you have the heroic inspiration
to bash your full belly
upon a hard rock? So!
Since I didn't want to see
the sun
Since I didn't want this miserable life.
Since I suffer so much, so...
Oh, mother, are you crying?
And why?
Are you feeling regret
for having created me?
Are you imagining the harm
that torments and shatters me
so terribly?
Oh, if only I had the strength
so that I could curse you...
But no!
No! No! No!
I am too cowardly!

The river flows and sings...
(the beautiful, peaceful, laughing river).
It flows over its fine bed
of soft sand
and its white froth
is tufted with gold.

The titanic cliff
bathes its granite flanks
in your clear waters
—oh, solitary river—
and seated at your edge I
watch the green leaves
that the wind caresses,
embroidered with shadow and light. So!
I watch. I think and remember...
But my mind is gloomy,
and all around me,
the evening weeps. Black.
I no longer love.
I no longer believe!

Who?
Who has ever caused me so much harm?
Women and love?
Men and friendship?
Society and its laws?
Humanity and its faith?
Maybe all of them!
Maybe none of them!
I don't know...
I feel much too bad...
Too much! Too much! Too much!
Here... in my mind!

My Demon sleeps
He sleeps in the gloomy twilight
of this mind of mine.
How sad I am...
Sad and melancholy.

I want new friends.
Real new friends.
I need to confide
my black melancholy
(in someone).
But I have no friends
I am alone!
Alone with my MELANCHOLY
Alone with my Destiny.
Alone, so alone!

My Demon sleeps.
A Memory passes
through my brain.
The Memory of a dream.
I dream of youth:
Strong, happy men
embraced, intertwined
with the naked bodies
of beautiful, joyful, happy women
celebrated and glorified
by happy, innocent children.
Then:
Flowers and sun.
Music and dance.
Stars and poetry.
Songs and love.

My Demon sleeps.
Dull yellow, black,
and greenish flashes
of foul reality
pass through my brain!

Flashes of the reality that is passing…
A mixture of brutes and boors.
A mixture of hypocrisy and ignorance.
A blending of cowardice and lies.
A totality of dung and mud.
Oh, no!
No! No! No!
I suffer too much!
Too much! Too much! Too much!

The sun has set
(the beautiful, golden sun)
The Angels of the evening
are in their death throes…
The green leaves are cold,
laughing dead skulls…
The river (the beautiful, clear river)
is now a black serpent
fearfully stretched out
between the cliff boulders.
Gloomy, silent grave.
Gloomy, black grave.
My cigarette is used up…
(my cigarette as pale
and hot as an ailing lover).
The ash has dispersed
along with the smoke.
There is nothing left for me
but a bit of yellow nicotine
on my bitter lips:
like life and dreams. So!

I go into the gloomy twilight

of my mind
my red Demon awakens.
I feel a tiny trickle of bitter blood
flowing over my bitter lips...
I have a tragic premonition
What will happen tonight?
But... the stars
—the dear stars—
will see.
If only I could laugh
and curse once more...
But I see a sinister lamp (a fire?)
shining in the darkness of the night.
I will have to STRIKE! I feel it...
I feel it! I feel it! I feel it!
I am a star that is turning toward a tragic sunset.

Weeping

[Due to wartime censorship some parts
are missing.—translator]

Weeping!

[censored]

...

And the "few" were ours... They were ours and fallen... How many of ours have fallen?

How many of them will yet fall?

These are the two terrible questions that lock our throats in a sob and that fill our hearts with weeping!

Oh, it's not true, no! that weeping is always "christian." There are times in life—agonizing, heart-breaking times— in which weeping is only for the strong, the bold, those who desperately swim against the torrent...

Oh, they are fallen, these "few"! Fallen in the bloody mud of the trenches, with hearts shattered by the murderous powder and iron... And yet enclosed within these fine and generous hearts there was a thoroughly superb and magnificent dream of love...

But this is just "sentimentalism from madmen and visionaries," isn't it true, oh former comrades of yesterday?

Oh, if we even considered you worthy of our contempt!

If we could still honor you with our whip!

But you have gathered the mire, with which you have replaced your brain and your heart, into swamps too noxious for you to even be able to deserve all this!

[censored]

... But this is still and always "petty moralizing by priestlike bigots and philosophasters,"[2] isn't it true, oh excellent renegades?

---

2   Here Novatore uses a few neologisms. The actual phase reads: "*moralina da pretonzoli e da filosofastri.*" It is clear that Novatore is playing

74

Ah, triply vile!

But at least don't delude yourselves about being Nietzsche's or Stirner's followers, oh useless Rabagas,[3] oh various anarchoids like Tancredi[4] or Nerucci[5]; put aside this supreme insult to these two stark shades of thinkers who knew how to bring a powerful breath of innovation into the boundless field of philosophy; while you have never been anything but their apers and what you've said and written has been nothing but a repugnant caricature and a foul parody.

But we, we repeat, can no longer have words for you! In this gloomy night, saturated with collective madness, we think of out fallen "few," and for them we pour out all our bitterest tears in torrents!

DE PROFUNDIS!

Yes, we pour out all our bitterest tears in torrents! But our tears fall—like a beneficial dew on golden crops— into the clear chalices of the Future, through which the radiant light of a new day already shines!

We are those who, born in the present, live in the future: you are the leftover stock of a medieval past that the tumultuous waves

---

on "morality" ("*morale*" in Italian), "priest" ("prete" in Italian), and "philosopher" ("*filososo*") in Italian. "Filosofastro" is also a play on "*poetastro*" which translates as poetaster, an insulting term for one who makes a pretense of being a poet while having no capacity for writing poetically. Thus, philosophasters would be those who make a pretense of being philosophers while having no capacity for deep thought—[translator's note].

3   A reference to Victorien Sardou's play *Rabagas* about a Monacan demagogue, a revolutionary politico who changes sides to get a bit of power.

4   Libero Tancredi (real name, Massimo Rocca), a former individualist anarchist who later became a fascist. He published the magazine *Novatore*. Between 1915 and 1918, he supported the war, and a few years later he joined Mussolini. He was the most famous of the individualists who became fascists.

5   Another turncoat, Raffaele Nerucci had been anarchist, came out in support of the first world war in 1915, and later joined Mussolini's fascists. Many comrades were sure that Nerucci worked for the police even before he became an interventionist.

of history have tumbled up to our times so that we can witness the magnificent funeral that accompanies your whole semi-barbaric bourgeois-christian and... democratic civilization to its tomb.

Oh, how fatal History is... She hast wanted—with a tragic and magnificent play—to place the spade in your hand with which you have to dig your grave yourself...

She cries out the DE PROFUNDIS of all your traditional ideals in a great voice, and your decrepit society tormenting itself in cruel pangs of the most atrocious agony, and around its bed of turpitude and degeneration stand grinning skulls in thousands and millions!

But while they grin these skulls speak a strange language that you can't and don't want to understand, but that we will explain to you tomorrow... Tomorrow... But today?... Today there is nothing left for us but weeping... weeping for our fallen "few"!

GERMINAL! The sun will return to the earth! He the protector and friend of the passionate lovers of Light!

The Sunrise will kill the gloomy children of the Night!

It isn't for them that the virgin Dawn breaks!

Oh, sunrise! Dawn! Sun! Noon!

GERMINAL! This is the fateful cry in which the voice of the Genius and that of the Hero fuse and merge in order to dissolve in unity in a tremulous song that, repeating "echo" after "echo," through the night of the Centuries, runs in an endless gallop toward the Infinite, toward the Universal, toward Eternity!

GERMINAL! This is the Altar on which true Heroes are sacrificed!

This is the magnificent, unpolluted garden where from the "sublime Lucretius"—as Leopardi described him—to all the various geniuses of ancient Hellenism, they cast the first seeds of the flowers of the future and where the "great German rebel" cast the seed that gave fruit to the "Unique ones," the "Free," the "Iconoclasts."

And here is Nietzsche, the barbarian who goes mad to teach people to go beyond themselves, to push them toward the highest peaks, in the face of strong winds where only the PURE can survive, those who are able to understand the superb feast, celebrated in the midst of magnificent and natural beauty!

And Tolstoy? Here is one who spread Love with full hands! Here is one who wanted to teach people to free themselves from a world full of abject malice and abominable cowardice!

And Proudhon? And Schopenhauer? Rousseau, Rèclus, Gori, Ferrer? And many others?

Oh, how many, how many cried out: GERMINAL!

And the Poets? And the Artists? Here is Oscar Wilde!

Here is one who lived wrapped up in a magnificent dream of beauty, and through the polyphonic symphony of his Art a new world shines through, unfortunately still unknown and ignored by almost all those who experience our work!

And Ibsen? And the author of *The Flowers of Evil*?

And Shelley? And Zola?

Oh, how many! How many, by different and opposing paths, have run toward the supreme synthesis, toward the great Noon, while, accompanied by the lacerating notes of Richard Wagner, they cry out: GERMINAL!

And Germinal!

The condemnation of an entire shameful past that crumbles miserably and that History overwhelms in the frightful shadow of time!

And we Germinal! We have incised it in our hearts!

Il Libertario, vol.XV, no.686, La Spezia, February 15

1919

Anarchist Individualism in the Social Revolution
written under the name of Mario Ferrento

Anarchist individualism as we understand it—and I say *we* because a substantial handful of friends think this like me—is hostile to every school and every party,

every churchly and dogmatic moral, as well as every more or less academic imbecility. Every form of discipline, rule, and pedantry is repulsive to the sincere nobility of our vagabond and rebellious restlessness!

Individualism is, for us, creative force, immortal youth, exalting beauty, redemptive and fruitful war. It is the marvelous apotheosis of the flesh and the tragic epic of the spirit. Our logic is that of not having any. Our ideal is the categorical negation of all other ideals for the greatest and supreme triumph of the actual, real, instinctive, reckless, and merry life! For us perfection is not a dream, an ideal, a riddle, a mystery, a sphinx, but a vigorous and powerful, luminous and throbbing reality. All human beings are perfect in themselves. All they lack is the heroic courage of their perfection. Since the time that human beings first believed that life was a duty, a calling, a mission, it has meant shame for their power of being, and in following phantoms, they have denied themselves and distanced themselves from the real. When Christ said to human beings: "be yourselves, perfection is in you!" he launched a superb phrase that is the supreme synthesis of life.

It is useless that the bigots, theologians, and philosophers do their utmost with deceitful and dialectical sophisms to give a false interpretation to Christ's words. But when Christ speaks this way to human beings, he disavows his entire calling to renunciation, to a mission, and to faith, and all the rest of his doctrine collapses miserably in the mud, knocked down by he himself. And here, and here alone, is Christ's great tragedy. Let human beings open their misty eyes in the blinding sun of this truth, and they will find themselves face to face with their true and laughing redemption.

This is the ethical part of individualism, neither romantically mystical nor idealistically monastic, neither moral nor immoral, but amoral, wild, furious, and warlike, that keeps its luminous roots voluptuously rooted in the phosphorescent perianth of pagan nature, and its verdant foliage resting on the purple mouth of virgin life.

2

To every form of human Society that would try to impose renunciations and artificial sorrow on our anarchic and rebellious I, thirsting for free and exulting expansion, we will respond with a roaring and sacrilegious howl of dynamite.

To all those demogogues of politics and of philosophy that carry in their pockets a beautiful system made by mortgaging a corner of the future, we respond with Bakunin: *Oafs and weaklings!* Every duty that they would like to impose on us we will furiously trample under our sacrilegious feet. Every shady phantom that they would place before our eyes, greedy for light, we will angrily rip up with our daringly profaning hands. Christ was ashamed of his own doctrine and he broke it first. Friedrich Nietzsche was afraid of his overhuman and made it die in the midst of his agonizing animals, asking pity of the higher man. But we are neither afraid nor ashamed of the liberated Human Being.

We exalt Prometheus, the sacrilegious thief who stole the eternal spark from Jove's heaven to animate the man of clay, and we glorify Hercules, the powerful, liberating hero.

3

Pagan nature has placed a Prometheus in the mind of every mortal human being, and a Hercules in the brain of every thinker. But morality, that disgusting enchantress of philosophers, peoples, and humanity, has glorified and sanctified the vulture exalting it as divine justice, and divine justice, which Comte humanized, has condemned the Hero.

The Plowman and the thinker have trembled before this baleful phantom and courage has remained defeated under the enormous weight of fear.

But anarchist individualism is a brilliant and fatal torch that casts light into the darkness in the realm of fear and puts to flight the phantoms of divine justice that Comte humanized.

Individualism is the free and unconstrained song that reconnects the individual to the eternal and universal pandynamism, that is neither moral nor immoral, but that is everything: Nature and Life! What is Life? Depths and peaks, instinct and reason, light and darkness, mud and beauty, joy and sorrow. Disavowal of the past, domination of the present, longing and yearning for the future.

Life is all this. And all this is also individualism. Who seeks to escape Life? Who dares to deny it?

4

The Social Revolution is the sudden awakening of Prometheus after a fall into a faint of sorrow caused by the foul vulture that rips his heart to shreds. It is an attempt at self-liberation. But the chains with which the sinister god Jove had him chained on the Caucasus by the repugnant servant Vulcan cannot be broken except by the Titanic rebel Hero, son of Jove himself.

We rebel children of this putrid humanity that has chained human beings in the dogmatic mud of social superstitions will never miss bringing our tremendous axe blow down on the rusty links of this hateful chain.

Yes, we anarchist individualists are for Social Revolution, but in our way, it's understood!

The revolt of the individual against society is not given by that of the masses against governments. Even when the masses submit to governments, living in the sacred and shameful peace of their resignation, the anarchist individual lives against society because he is in a never-ending and irreconcilable war with it, but when, at a historical turning point, he comes together with the masses in revolt, he raises his black flag with them and throws his dynamite with them.

The anarchist individualist is in the Social Revolution, not as a demagogue, but as a inciting element, not as an apostle, but as a living, effective, destructive force...

All past revolutions were, in the end, bourgeois and conservative. That which flashes on the red horizon of our magnificently tragic time will have for its aim the fierce socialist humanism. We, anarchist individualists, will enter into the revolution for an exclusive need of our own to set fire to and incite spirits. To make sure that, as Stirner says, it is not a new revolution that approaches, but rather an immense, proud, reckless, shameless, conscienceless crime that rumbles with the lightning on the horizon, and beneath which the sky, swollen with foreboding, grows dark and silent. And Ibsen: *There's only one revolution I recognize—that was truly, thoroughly radical—... I'm referring to the ancient Flood! That one alone was truly serious. But even then the devil lost his due: you know Noah took up the dictatorship. Let's make this revolution again, but more thoroughly. It requires real men as well as orators. So you bring on the roaring waters, I'll supply the powder keg to blow up the ark.*

Now since dictatorship will be—alas!—inevitable in the somber global revolution that sends its bleak glow from the east over our black cowardice, the ultimate task of we anarchist individualists will be that of blowing up the final ark with bomb explosions and the final dictator with Browning shots. The new society established, we will return to its margins to live our lives dangerously as noble criminals and audacious sinners! Because the anarchist individualist still means eternal renewal, in the field of art, thought, and action.

Anarchist individualism still means eternal revolt against eternal sorrow, the eternal search for new springs of life, joy and beauty. And we will still be such in Anarchy.

Il Libertario, vol.VXI, no.738 & 739, November 6 & 13

The Great (?) Brains... in the Time that Turns
written under the name of Mario Ferrante

FRATERNALLY REMEMBERING
OTTAVIO TOGNELLI E CARLO MOLASCHI

> *To the one who has experienced much and not*
> *committed suicide, giving him death as*
> *a reward is not a splendid human act.*
> —Renzo Novatore

I confess that I have never managed to explain to myself Renzo Novatore very well how human beings (who they want to call genius...) have always been so slow and retrograde, reactionary and ignorant about social questions. Look a bit at that nut-case Giovanni Papini for example!

He who is a bold and original navigator among the tardy waves roaring in the immense ocean of philosophy and human thought, who knows how to dive into the most frightening and deepest whirlpools singing lyrically in order to bring back to the dwellers on the shore the most precious jewels in bloodstained hands; look a bit, I said, at the above-mentioned man, how does he become ridiculous, and superficially and crudely vulgar when he tries to concern himself with politics and economy?

It's a thing that will have made you weep from laughter if you have followed the evolutionary involution of this most unhappy man!

Let's perhaps forget now that his tired and finished brain decomposes and rots like a mushroom that has lived too long under the strong downpours of November. But earlier? It has nearly always been this way!

And D'Annunzio? Will you look a bit also at him as he dizzily rushes toward the sublime peaks of the *shit-hole* now? Alright, so he too is rotten and finished. But, in the past? About social questions (remember?) he has always been so stupid one can only pity him! And yet there was genius (no more now of any evaluation, of him as of the others) in that brain, there's no denying it... When he entered into the garden of Art, he offered us certain bouquets of flowers, that despite the sharp scent, a bit perverse (and not just in the bourgeois sense) and a bit too much sexually lascivious, one felt hidden in it a mystical and modest pulse of heroic and superhuman beauty! And then? And then it is this way. It is this way also with Benedetto Croce, you see. He (though for me he is the most gentlemanly slanderer of the Aesthetic) is also one of the boldest personalities on the not very glorious field of Italian culture. And yet do you at all observe how ridiculous he also is when he arms himself with all his colossal political ignorance to descend to do battle in the field of social questions?

But what could one ever make of these distinguished names, all deficient, some more, some less, from this weakness?

If you want to go from the field of the living to the field of the dead, it would be the chance to immediately encounter F. Nietzsche himself, the satanic, playfully destructive philosopher, saturated with desperately and divinely creative, intoxicating poetry, discoverer of the strangest and most original truths of the human mind—well, he himself, I said, when he tried to concern himself with social questions was seized by the same myopia, by that same weakness: which one might call: *The ignorance of great men!* and in that book of his... *Beyond Good and Evil*, he sought to create (though under a formula all his own) a certain legislative theory for the use and consumption of a certain aristocracy (which I would call imperialistic) that he invented at the complete and exclusive injury of the people.

And saying that it would be enough that the people went to quench their thirst (oh! if they only had thirst...) at the springs of Nietzschean philosophy to throw it all into the air in an absolute and radical way both in the spiritual realm and in that of this materialistically experienced life of ours... Yes, precisely this, all in the air including his theory of aristocratic (thus not very aristocratic in the libertarian sense) domination!

In this instance Stirner himself seems more noble, more logical, and less cruel to me...

In fact on social questions, if it were granted to me to give advice to the great men, I would say (at least to those who are still living, and who still know how to read) to go back a bit to read that little, but so valuable, booklet that is called *The Soul of Man Under Socialism*, author Oscar Wilde who is more than one of their peers... But perhaps it is useless to make predictions about this since, alas!, there must be a certain fatality that weighs on all things. Even on the brains of the great men... With all this, however, I can't yet close this topic without adding something else that is perhaps what matters most. And that is to explain, from my point of view, the psychology of this ugly affair.

It is, I believe, and I don't just believe, I'm sure , that the phenomenon is explained like this. The great man, by his nature, lives in the world of his own greatness, meaning outside of the life of the people. Two lives, two worlds, two realities, and also two faults, this: that the people still haven't learned how to become deserving of the name that they bear, that is: real people. The great men that of not having learned how to become truly great. Meaning that they still have to learn to not stick their so keenly delicate nose into the affairs of the people. Politics is a low, vulgar thing, linked to the economy, or rather is the economy itself. Now the economic affair, being an affair of the belly and of the kitchen, is important, indispensable, the most indispensable of all, but an affair for cooks, so not for poets and higher men.

What addle-brained mania draws you to go down from the fifth floor to the kitchen? Are you perhaps afraid that that bit of fuel for making your fantastic and beautiful machine function will be lacking for you? Are you possibly by chance among the followers of the belly, even you, oh higher men? I don't want to believe it... And then?

Well then I'll explain things this way, oh dear men who inhabit the high astral spheres, and who I admire as one admires the sun when you stay there superbly in your magic realm. But precisely because you are minds and spirits, the kitchen is not your affair. You, if you are truly great men, should give the people your superfluous splendor just like the sun. But don't come down anymore, for God's sake! You only muddle things up. To your honor, I tell you that you are too far away from the life of the people to be able to understand which flavorings are best to put into the pot to make the finest soup.

Every time that the bad idea has sprung into one of your heads to act as a cook, either the pot has broken, or the fire has gone out, or something worse has happened...

No, you are great... I tell you again, and you could never understand what is below! So stay there in your realm, this will be your most beautiful glory, your most beautiful virtue, and also your best *health*... You see, in this amorphous and deformed monster that is called "People" (the bourgeoisies excluded because I believe that even for you it must by now be a nauseating and repugnant subspecies) it is still necessary for us to recognize once and for all one of its special practical and political virtues, that, thanks to Lenin and not only to him, it is learning magnificently. Yes, the social question is a vulgar, not very artistic female, but she is its, exclusively its: of the people!

Why do you want to snatch it from them? Don't you have your beautiful and seductive women in your own realm, made and molded of splendor and light? The people has in its proletarian ranks philosophers (working class philosophers) who especially now will well know how to look after and guide their females. But then, for good or ill, it is a thing that shouldn't interest you who are of another world... What does it matter to the sun whether it sends out its rays over a murky or a clear sea? It throws its superfluous splendor (true treasure of its higher and lordly wealth) and moves on! Yes, I say it to you, in the field of social politics the people will be a superior cultivator, very superior to you. It will understand now the reality of its life, which is not yours. It will take with it experience, boldness, and knowledge, and it will guide itself well. When you try to go down (and to your shame) into this field of things, you give me the impression of one of those children of this democratically modern fatal aristocracy, that having suddenly become (?) stupid and vulgar, rushes with proud and childish arrogance into the hovel of *his* peasant and in the name of his *nobility* tries to seduce the most beautiful, elder daughter, under the pretext that doing so honors and elevates her...

It's true (unfortunately, I know it) that females are females, and that often times they allow themselves to be seduced by this so very little noble and gentlemanly manner, but it is also true that sometimes they scratch, and the female's fingernails are poisonous, gentlemen, and leave certain cursed wounds that deform the face; and that's not all! Without considering then that one runs the risk of seeing a rough and robust shepherd (the working class philosopher) suddenly come out of the stall, who, armed with a knotty cudgel, gives a grim, well-aimed blow into the brain (that's right... precisely into the brain!) of the dolled up and noble seducer sending him to end up no longer in the world of the sun or that of the earth, that of the people or that of the nobility, but in a third world.

Into the one, that is to say, that Dante has already made "Panders, and barrators[6], and the like-filth" inhabit, and where one already finds that putrid, mediocre, and stupid pack of morally, spiritually, and psychically depraved people, spies, pederasts, rotten, and corrupt people. That correspond to the sectarian and

6   The term "barrator" refers to one who habitually incites disputes or legal actions—often frivolous or malicious in nature.

despicable names of Libero Tancredi[7], Maria[8] (the deceitful and depraved spy), the vulgar adventurer Benito Mussolini, and all the other filthy pigs of red interventionism. And doing this, the rough shepherd (the working class philosopher)—now bolshevik— is sacredly right. The one who, in the name of refined and higher aristocratic nobility, doesn't want to lower himself to the "sickening stench" that emanates from the house of the people, not even when, like now, Spring, Sun, and the *germination* of roses is there... in order to then go down at night to see when he'd be able to ravish and corrupt the wife, he lowers himself to the action of an alcoholic municipal garbage man and something worse... If he were at least guided by a passion; then...

But then... it is a shame, a rotten shame I tell you, oh higher men... I admire and discover myself in front of those who remain always in the heights. The true children of the sun, but you, oh Croce Benedetto[9], oh Papini Giovanni[10], oh D'Annunzio Gabriele, oh Benelli Sam[11], and your other little apes, disgust me, simply disgust me!

You should now be made to climb the "electric chair" of rude, lacerbian memory, first of all its inventor, but it would be more

---

7   The *nom de plume* of Massimo Rocca, involved in the anarchist movement in the early 1900s. Around 1911, he began advocating "proletarian nationalism." He supported "interventionism" in World War I (ie, he had a pro-war view) and eventually joined the fascists, but was exiled for taking a "revisionist" view on fascist violence.
8   Maria Ryger (1885-1953) was a militant woman who first supported socialism, then anarchism (anti-militarism), then interventionism, then fascism, then democracy, then monarchy.
9   Benedetto Croce (1866-1952) is one of the best-known Italian philosophers, and was one of the founders of the Italian Liberal Party.
10   Giovanni Papini (1881-1956) was a futurist writer. In his youth, he was iconoclastic and rebellious, but he went on to support the war and fascism, and became part of academia.
11   Sam Benelli (1877-1949) was a famous writer who, at one time, wrote for anarchist papers, but then went on to support the war and join the fascists. Because Mussolini didn't like him, like Tancredi, he had problems under the fascist regime.

hygienic to make you climb the one that the *great* American pal keeps in his house.[12]

But let's see! One never knows in these marvelous times of *Bolshevism* how it will end up... Because among all the other good intentions there is in us also that of being, at least once, deeply human toward those who have experienced too much.

It's not enough that there is the kingly freedom of suicide... something more is wanted! And the red wind of the east will bring that something more!

Do you feel that scent in the air?

Spring is coming! Already one can see all around a "rosy pallor"—says comrade Tognetti—"that sweetly transforms into yellow orange and then into flaming red" and it is "The Vermillion Dawn". Hail!, oh, Ottavio, we will soon have the Midday Sun.

Il Libertario, vol.VXI, no.711, April 24

---

12   *Lacerba* was a futurist magazine published by Giovanni Papini in 1913. It included a regular review column called "Electric Chair" with violent, scathing polemical reviews against the people and works of academia.

Returning

Dear *Libertario*, twenty-two months have passed since the day that the most brutal and slimiest of all monsters tried to crush me between its filthy and bloody jaws.

Yes, I too was destined to be transformed into a humble tool of bestial slavery; I too was destined to be sacrificed (O sacrificial animals…) on the altar of the stupidest, most grotesque of all human phantasms; I also was destined to be transformed into a "piece of human material"… But I don't believe in destiny.

Nor do I believe in fatality. No! I only believe in the capacity of my power! And only in its name did I respond in a refined anarchist way, with a superb and scornful "NO."

And I took off…

I walked with infinite joy on the paths of Sorrow.

I always had danger as my companion, like a dear brother. On my lips, I always had the smile of the highest, strong beings; in my calm eyes, the fascinating vision of the heroic tragedy that only true lovers of free life understand.

I was alone… but I knew that a daring phalanx of the coherent and bold remained hidden in the shadows, living the same life as me. Ah, how much love I felt for this nameless group…

What did it matter if many of them languished for so long in the depths of a damp cell? They didn't submit! They lived; we will live at the margins of society as true rebels, as intransigent Iconoclasts, not caring what the final tragedy might be.

And it is to this handful of conscious "dark protestors," oh dear *Libertario*, that I send through your columns—after deeply thanking you and all the groups of anarchist comrades and socialist friends for the greatest moral and material solidarity given to me during my illegal wandering and my…legal imprisonment—my most fervent and fraternal greetings, saying to them: *Be proud of your actions, because only through disobedience and revolt is a*

brilliant ray of human beauty born!
A salute to you, oh anarchists of the deed!
A salute to you, oh human brothers!

Il Libertario, no.732, La Spezia, September 25

The Expropriator

My freedom and my right are as great as the
capacity of my power. I will also have happiness
and greatness to the extent of my strength.
(FROM A BOOK I WROTE THAT WILL NEVER SEE THE LIGHT.)

The Expropriator is the most beautiful, manly, uninhibited, virile figure that I have ever met in anarchism. He is the one who waits for nothing. He is the one who has no altar on which to sacrifice himself. He glorifies life alone with the philosophy of Action.

I came to know him on a distant August afternoon while the sun embroidered verdant nature in gold as, perfumed and festive, she sang a merry song of pagan beauty.

He told me: *I was always a restless, vagabond, rebellious spirit.*

I studied men and their minds in books and in reality. I found them to be a mixture of the comical, the vulgar, and the cowardly. They left me nauseous. On the one hand, baleful moral phantoms, created from the lies and hypocrisy that rule. On the other hand, sacrificial animals who worship with fanaticism and cowardice. This is the world of men. This is humanity. I feel revulsion for this world, for these men, for this humanity. Plebeians and bourgeois are the same. They deserve each other. Socialism would not agree. It has discovered **good** *and* **evil**. *And to destroy these two antagonisms, it has created two more phantoms:* **Equality** *and* **Fraternity** *among men...*

But men will be equal before the state and free under Socialism... Socialism has given up Force, Youth, War! But when the bourgeoisie, who are spiritual beggars, don't want to see themselves as equals of the rabble, who are material beggars, then even sniveling socialism allows war. Yes, even socialism allows killing and expropriating. But in the name of an ideal of human equality and fraternity... that sacred equality and fraternity that began with Cain and Abel!...

But with socialism one only half-thinks; one is half-free; one lives by half!... Socialism is intolerance; it is impotence of living; it is faith in fear. I go beyond!

Socialism has found equality **good** *and inequality* **evil**. *Slaves good and tyrants wicked. I have crossed the threshold of good and evil in order to live my life intensely. I live today and cannot wait for tomorrow. Waiting is for the people and for humanity, therefore it cannot be my affair. The future is fear's mask. Courage and strength have no future for the simple reason that they themselves are the future that turns on the past and destroys it.*

Life's purity goes on only with the nobility of courage that is the philosophy of action.

I observe: *The purity of this life of yours seems to me to border on crime!*

He responds: *Crime is the highest synthesis of freedom and life. The moral world is a world of phantoms. Here there are specters and the specters' shadows; here there is the Ideal, universal Love, the Future. Look, the specters' shadow: ignorance, fear, and cowardice lie there. Deep darkness, perhaps eternal. I once also lived in that gloomy, filthy prison. Then I armed myself with a sacrilegious torch, setting fire to phantoms and violating the night. When I reached the gates of good and evil, I furiously tore them down and crossed their threshold.*

The bourgeoisie has launched its moral anathema, the idiotic rabble its moral curse, at me.

But both are humanity. I am a man. Humanity is my enemy. It wants to clasp me in a thousand horrid tentacles. I try to snatch all that my yearnings need from it. We are at war.

All that I have the strength to snatch away from it is mine. And I sacrifice all that is mine on the altar of my life and my freedom. This life of mine that I feel throbbing amidst the pulsing flames that blaze in my heart; amidst the wild agony of my entire being that fills my mind with divine upheavals and creates thunderous fanfares of war and polyphonic symphonies of a higher, strange, and unknown love which echo in my spirit. This life that fills my veins with vigorous and lively blood that spreads diabolical spasms of exultant expansion through all my muscles, nerves, and flesh; spasms of this life of mine that I glimpse through the crazed vision of my dreams, eager and in need of endless development. My motto is: to go along expropriating and burning, always leaving cries of moral outrage and smoking trunks of ancient things behind me.

When men no longer possess ethical wealth—the only treasures that are truly inviolable—then I will throw away my lock picks. When there are no longer phantoms in the world, then I will throw away my torch. But this future is far away and may never come! And I am a child of this distant future, fallen into this world by Chance, to whose power I bow.

So the Expropriator told me on that distant August afternoon, while the sun embroidered verdant nature in gold as, perfumed and festive, she sang a merry song of pagan beauty.

Iconoclasta!, No.10, Pistoia, November 26

Toward the Hurricane

While it is day we will remain
with head high and everything
that we can do we will not leave
before we have done it.
—W. Goethe

We heat our pen in the volcanic fire of our negating spirit. We dip it in our vigorous heart, full of rebellious blood. And in the atheistic light of our mind, we write and write...

So we write, quickly, without literary pursuits, without repugnant theoretical ideologies, without bigoted and sentimental mush from hysterics and political hacks, wrapped only in the cloak of our raging passions.

We write only words of blood, fire, and light.

My rough, fiery, energetic pen creaks and scrapes over the white purity of this page, like a viper's tongue over the tender throat of an innocent baby, giving it death, through poison.

Away, away from me, all ideologies, theosophies, dogmatic and political philosophies; far from me, all preestablished systems: everything has fallen and burned to ashes in the corroding flame of my negating spirit.

I am the complete nihilist, the radical atheist.

I did not just now find out, I did not just now discover and come to know that the one and only most beautiful frame-work within which proud human Individuality stands out free, solemn, and magnificent is Nothing, the true Nothing!

No foul prison could ever hold this rebellious, iconoclastic spirit of mine; now less than ever!

Now that the enormous trumpet of time has sounded—and indeed it has sounded strong blasts to break the hardest neck of the idiotic rabble—the bold phalanges of black flame must furiously spring forth from Nothing. In the passionate violence of spontaneous revolt, this flame will form the crackling pillar of fire which goes before the people, giving the first warning of final destruction. This is the hour of feverish bitterness, of terrible anguish!

This is the hour that comes before the divine hour of imminent tragedy, which will give us heroic Death and heroic Greatness.

Oh delightful hour that gives me all the feverish intensity of spirit, I love you!

I would not give up all the bitterness that you bring me for all the mediocre sweetness in the world. I would not give up the fevers that hammer my temple, that burn my temples, that burn my forehead for the tranquility and peace of all the cowardly men.

Oh, Satan, inspire me! Inspire me, oh my divine brother!

Give me the hellish potential to set fire to all those virgin spirits that have not yet been buried in the dung heap of deceitful theories; make it possible for me to draw a daring handful of lovers of heroic, libertarian Greatness and Heroic Death close to me.

But they will be there! They must be there! May the temperate souls remain calmly rotting away in the company of their stupid saints and senile, old, good god.

But we will march! The time has come for all those who, by dominating the ideal, have become its symbol and embodiment to march.

Wrapped in the divinity of our torment, we will go forward and, through the example of our deeds, we will show people which paths lead to new light. Will we fall? It doesn't matter! We want liberation from the stupid life of humility, slavery, servility, where man must walk on his knees and the spirit must speak in a subdued, low voice, like a prayer.

It is necessary to kill christian philosophy in the most radical sense of the word. The more it goes slinking into democratic civilization (this most cynically ferocious form of christian corruption), the more it becomes the categorical negation of human

Individuality.

Democracy! Now we know that it means all this. Oscar Wilde said that democracy is "the bludgeoning of the people, by the people, for the people".

The hour for rising up against all this has sounded and not just with some disagreeable and repugnant theoretical sheep's bleating.

Something else entirely is wanted in this bloody twilight of a civilization whose time is over! Either Death or a new Dawn where Individuality lives above every thing.

I have forgotten everything, or rather, not forgotten, but gone beyond (and I know with how much torment), even the unsurpassable love for my Mate and the adoration for my child.

My books—my dear books that I loved above all else— now rest far away from me, there in the old house, in a large chest of drawers, maybe covered in dust, maybe bathed with the tears of my dear Mate.

But even my love for you, my dear books, luminous torch of my thoughts, is overcome!

Today, I feel something inside me, stronger than any love, something that kisses my mind with all the heat of an irresistible charm...

On the ruins of all this that I destroyed through negation, a new faith is reborn. Faith in the impossible made possible by my negation, or the final purification, how very real, that is met among the ardent flames of the final, tragic and redemptive catastrophe.

Today, I seek a single hour of raging anarchy, and I will give all my dreams, all my loves, all my life, for that hour.

But that hour will come! Oh, when will it come! And if it should not come, I would willingly give myself over to the human-eating hands of the idiotic and brutal society that has already given me a magnificent death sentence (for recalling that I possess higher ideas that have the value of pointing out that the divine freedom of the I is something more beautiful and greater than its

100

brutal war), and I would cynically make them shoot me as a sign of the deepest contempt for myself and the unmentionable cowardice of every human being.

Greeting the revived *Libertario* and the next social insurrection, I fraternally clasp the hands of true rebels of all the various tendencies!

Today is the eve of Action! At the first spark I will be among you.

Il Libertario, vol.XVIII, no.721, La Spezia, February 27

1920

A Life

To the friends of *Nichilismo*.

Memories

> *My youth was just a dark hurricane*
> *passed through here and there by brilliant suns;*
> *the lightning and the rain wreaked so much havoc,*
> *that few vermilion fruits were left in my garden.*
> —Charles Baudelaire

In a distant spring, gleaming with green and sun, my youthful spirit wandered gently through the divine forests of the sky. One day, a sad day in autumn, it came back to me, disconsolate, weeping. A groups of Angels with large, black wings accompanied it silently. It told me: "God is dead! The great Pan is dead!" The Sun went dark, rivers filled with mud, and plants trembled. Darkness wrapped the Earth in her funeral shroud. Then at my back I heard the satanic thunder of a hellish laugh. It was the laughter of he for whom I had waited, perhaps unaware, for so long: the Demon. He told me: "Come with me!" He brought me into the corrupt city where the *true* sun has never laid its kiss.

Dance of specters. Darkness. Silence... Beside a temple built for the Goddess of Perversity and Knowledge, a Fountain of Blood gurgled, as if reciting a cursed prayer.

The Demon was somber and black like the tragic Night. From his yellow, phosphorous eyes a ray of sinister light flowed.

Suddenly he told me "Goodbye!" and quickly vanished.

I cried out. I was alone in the deepest darkness. The Fountain continued to recite its cursed prayer. Did I tremble? Maybe. I don't know... I don't recall... Suddenly the gates of the temple of the Goddess of Perversity and Knowledge flew open and the

Fountain of Blood transmuted into the beautiful body of a voluptuous young woman.

"I love you"—she told me—"and I want you. You have to be mine!" I looked into the depth of her eyes. I recognized her. She was the Image perceived through a morbid dream of Matter. A hellish mob blossomed from my mind, inspiring in me a Dionysian quiver.

"Matter is everything!" I forgot the place and time and tried to catch that naked and beautiful body so I could take it in my arms and grasp it tightly to my breast.

"No, not here!..." she told me. And taking my hot and feverish hand in her small, cool one, she led me through the flowery entrance of a cavern in which a group of young

witches danced. We abandoned ourselves to a wild embrace, and my large, gaping, passionate mouth enclosed her tiny, beautiful lips in a bite. We closed our eyes. In the midst of so much darkness, I noticed that my mind was not dead, since it had never seen a vaster sea of light.

I don't know how much time passed. I was suddenly roused by the roar of a funeral march echoing dismally from the bottom of the cavern. Laughing wildly, my companion told me: "The witches are dead. Our embrace killed them. I am avenged!" And saying this, she turned pale, stiffened and became a rock.

A young serpent with eyes of fire and a bloodstained mouth rose up before me: "You have brought death to my lovers and killed Love." "And what does that matter?" I answered. "I have known him a long time," I continued, "this hypocritical, cynical and cruel God of yours. I have seen him insult and mangle so many of my sisters. I have seen him—like all other Gods—shedding blood, devastating brains, feeding on young hearts, always for his own lustful body, in a hot bath of tears." The serpent bowed his head and said to me, "Look?!" and stuck his neck out at me. There he held the mirror of Life, upside-down. I looked into it and saw myself. In the mirror, I was nothing but a large skull. Thick black clouds lowered over my head. They were funeral hearses for my smothered dreams.

I saw my woman of stone nearly move.

Goblins loaded her onto a cloud that the wind drove into the heights and scattered in the distance.

Then the serpent's mouth vomited blood and made the ground open under my feet. I fell into a bottomless abyss.

Suspended in the void, I again saw the Demon.

"Brother, listen to me..." I said to him. And I whispered a few words in his ear.

Even he was pale, moved, and he answered me: "It is impossible to believe it. Ah, if I could do it!..."

Again my mind quivered. But then he suddenly burst out laughing. "What does it matter to you? Haven't you seen the mirror of Life?" He brought me by an unknown path and led me back to the magnificent Earth to mock Man, the Overman, the Demon, and God.

Torment

I know, how much pain and sweat and
baking sun it takes on the flaming hill
To engender my life and to give me soul
—Charles Baudelaire

Man, Demon and God have come together to defile my virgin garden. (I don't know why the Overman has not gotten there.) They are right in front of me like three perverse allegories. God tells me: "I am the unattainable good to which you should aspire. Sacrifice yourself, deny yourself, and you will reach me."

The Demon tells me: "I will give you happiness if you will worship me."

Man tells me: "I am the *Ideal* of atheists. Be me." I laugh. I laugh, but my laughter is not calm.

I feel that I am not Man, that I do not worship the Demon, that I do not sacrifice myself on the altar of any God; and yet, I still don't have the mathematical certainty of being my own I, the lord of my fantastic realm. This is my torment. When God tells me: "Killing is bad!"; when the Demon tells me: "Killing is necessary"; when Man tells me: "Great is the one who dies for the Ideal"; I answer each one of them: "That's not true!"

Someone knew that I loved conflict and said to me: "I have thousands of men with me, brave and valiant warriors,

we will win. Come with us." I asked him: "Why are you fighting?" "For the greatness of the Fatherland," he answered.

"I have no fatherland."

I met other men: "We know that you are a valiant warrior. Come with us. We will pour out our last drop of blood for the redemption of humanity."

I answered: "I don't believe in humanity, I don't believe in its redemption."

The group's leader scowled and looked at me with contempt: "You are a coward!"

I laugh. But my laughter still is not calm. I feel something bitter inside me that torments me.

I feel something inside me that is so deeply intimate that I don't know how to explain, that no one could ever explain. I feel within myself the UNSAYABLE!

It is *my unique self*, which no one knows. Is this perhaps my torment? Perhaps. Because perhaps it is my *Happiness*. Because perhaps it is the spring that quenches my thirst, that leads me to the final edge of the I which wants to expand itself and throb in the strong, vast spasm of the Everything, so as to dissolve triumphantly in the Nothing.

Flight

Must one depart? Or stay?...
If you can, stay; Depart, if you must.
—Charles Baudelaire

My arrow is ready, my will is rejuvenated, my potency proved. How could I wait any longer?

Yes, I must depart. It is time, it is time!

Nihil, nihil!

Tormented, my mind flies. It flies with the wings of Reality over the world of dreams, towards broader horizons, towards my eternity.

I can no longer dream, I am the dream of myself. The friend of my possible traveling companions.

•

Oh friends, oh friends, where are you?

Don't you see, over there, the Face of Eternity and Mystery? It is necessary to unravel the final riddle of the eternal.

Come on, friends, come, it is time, it is time!

...

Have you arrived?

I have never seen a sky as peaceful as your faces, oh friends.

How beautiful it is to understand each other.

•

We are on a frail boat, lost at sea. No more dawns, or dusks, or destinations. We have only sun, light, heat, depth and distance.

Do you hear? Eternity raises her most beautiful song to Life, as she demands of us the bridal rose garland. Oh friends, the roses, where are the roses?

•

What a poor, what a miserable thing the land where we lived was!

Do you still remember it, oh friends?

There golden dawns rose, but black nights fell…

There men dreamed of collective aims and measured time…

Ah, friends, friends, I am assailed by an immense pity for that poor land…

•

So what is happening to me?…

Let's forget it! For how many thousands of years have we floated on the endless waves of this vast depth that raises us to the regions of the Sun, above the Sun?

And for how many thousands of years will we yet live? Ah, jolly Eternity, eternal happy now!

•

May no one ever know the secret happiness that fills our solitary hearts, oh friends!

Have we not stoically suffered in forced silence?

No, no, may no one ever know our cruelest sorrows, nor the infinite happiness of this eternal noon.

In the grotesque old world, they now believe that we are dead.

And instead, we have married eternity, we—the loners!

—But the roses, oh friends? Where are the roses? Oh, red roses of Eternal Revolt!

Nichilismo, no.2, Milan April 20–May 5

The Anarchist Temperament
in the Maelstrom of History

In anarchism, beyond the two different philosophical concepts, the communistic and the individualistic, that divide it in the theoretical sphere, there are two spiritual and physical instincts—indeed, of life practically and materially experienced—which serve to distinguish two temperaments that are wholly common property to both theoretical and philosophical tendencies. Although both children of the same social suffering, we have two different instincts that give us two different forms of suffering, of hedonistic origin.

There are those (communists and individualists) who suffer—as Nietzsche would say—through an *over-abundance of life* and those who suffer from the *impoverishment of life*. Those communist and individualist lovers of quiet and peace, of silence and solitude, are among the latter. Those communists and individualists who feel their inner self as a mighty dionysian quiver overflowing with power, and life as heroic manifestation of force and will. They are the ones who have the instinctive and irresistable need to throw the flame of their "I" against the walls of the outer world to demolish and live the tragedy. We are among these!

We are in anarchism—first of all—from original instinct and passionate feeling. Our ideas are nothing other than bold and brilliant creatures born from the primitive monistic embrace with negating theoretical reason.

Today the history of humanity has reached one of its many maelstroms—perhaps the grandest—where the human spirit is called to radically renew itself on the magnificently horrendous ruins of fire and blood, catastophe and destruction, or cravenly crystallize itself in the decrepit and corpse-like concept of life that out-dated bourgeois society has dictated and imposed on us.

If a strong handful of rebels, higher people and heroes would be able to leap beyond the two currents of anarchism, suffering from vital over-abundance, to rally around the black flag of revolt, setting fire to the hearts of all the European nations, the old world would collapse, because around Heroes everything must fatefully transform into tragedy; and only in tragedy are born the renewing spirits that are able to hear, more nobly and highly, the festive song of their free life.

If this handful of daredevils will not leap out of the shadow to throw the black glove of defiance and revolt into the foul face of bourgeois society, the reptiles of politicalhack demagoguery and all the speculating acrobats and hypocrites of human sorrow will remain the masters of the field, and over the tragic sun that seeks to enlighten the dark maelstrom of the sombre history that is passing, they

will throw the obscene mask of white lead carried over the free horizon of human thought by that debauched clown named "Marx," and everything will end in a vile and grotesque comedy before which every anarchist should commit suicide out of dignity and shame.

For that portion of Italian anarchists who suffer from vital over-abundance; for that portion of Italian anarchists— individualist and communist—for whom battle, danger and tragedy are among their spiritual and material needs, the time has come!

The hour of imposing themselves and dominating. The true freedom and right of the human being is only in his capacity to WILL!

Right and freedom are Force!

What for others is painful sacrifice must be for us a gift and a joyous holocaust.

We need to throw ourselves on the wave of past time, tread the rounded tops of the centuries, manfully go back in history in order to drink at the virgin springs from which the blood of the first, free human sacrifices still gushes, hot and smoking.

We need to go back, barefoot and naked, among the living stones of the mythical, legendary forest and nourish ourselves, like our distant ancestors, on lion's marrow and on wild nature.

Only in this way—like Maria Vesta—will we be able to say to the first Hero who stoically and calmly knew how to offer his flesh to the red flames of a grim, crackling hostile blaze: Now we too, like you, can sing under torture.

The Life that society offers us in not a full, free and joyful life. It is a crushed, mutilated, humiliated life.

We must refuse it.

If we don't have the strength and ability to violently snatch from its hands the high and vigorous life that we so powerfully feel, let's throw this specter on the tragic altar of sacrifice and final renunciation.

At least we will be able to put a heroic crown of beauty on the bloody face of the art that enlightens and creates.

Better to rise on the flames of a fire and fall with broken skull under the volley of an unconscious firing squad than to accept this specter of ironic life, which is nothing more than a sinister parody of life.

Enough, oh friends, of cowardice. Enough, oh comrades, of the ingenuous illusion of the "generous act of the masses."

The mass is straw, is straw that socialism has put to rot in the stable of the bourgeoisie.

Errico Malatesta, Pasquale Binazzi, Dante Carnesecchi and thousands of others unknown who rot in those miasmal and deadly madhouses, which are the prisons of the Savoy monarchy and for which the small medal holders of the P.S.I. (Italian Socialist Party) have demanded at the parliamentary pigsty for the means to build others more vast, must for us be so many spectral regrets, walking in fearsome forms, among the uncertain twists and turns of our doubtful minds; they must be so many hot bursts of blood that break out from our hearts to shoot over the lines of our face and cover it with bleak shame.

I know, we know, that a hundred HUMAN BEINGS— deserving of this name—would be able to do what five hundred thousand unconscious "organized" ones are not and will never be capable of doing. Don't you see, oh friends, the shade of Bruno Filippi who sneers and watches us?

So are there no longer ONE HUNDRED ANARCHISTS in Italy deserving of this name? Are there no longer a hundred "I's" capable of walking with flaming feet over the whirling peaks of our ideas? Errico Malatesta and all the thousands of others who've fallen into the hands of the enemy at the first signs of this social storm, wait with noble and feverish eagerness the lightning that brings down the collapsing edifice, that illuminates history, that raises the values of life, that light the path of humanity...

But the brilliant and fateful lightning cannot break out from the heart of the masses.

The masses that seemed to be fervent admirers of Malatesta are cowardly and powerless.

The government and the bourgeoisie know it. They know and they sneer.

They know: "The P.S.I. is with us. It is the indispensable pawn for the baleful outcome of our wicked game. It is the Abracadabra that takes form in the Abracas and Abra voice of our magical, millenarian sorcery. The cowardly masses are its slaves and Errico Malatesta is old and sick. We will make him die in the hidden darkness of a damp cell, and later we will throw his corpse in the faces of his anarchist comrades...."

Yes, this is what the government and the bourgeoisie think in the hidden chambers of their idiotic and malicious minds. Do we want to bear this vile challenge with indifference? Do we want to bear this bloody and brutal insult in silence? Are we such cowards?

I hope that these three huge question marks of mine, so solemn and terrifying, will find in the ranks of anarchism a virile response that says: NO! With a terrible thundering still more terrible...

It is from the fiery summits of the luminous peaks that the liberating lightning must break forth.

The strong OLD MAN waits. Heroic comrades: TO US!

The corpse of an old agitator always costs more than the lives of a thousand malicious idiots.

Brothers and sisters, remember this.

Let's act so that the deepest of all human shame does not fall on us.

Il Libertario, vol.XVII, no.793, La Spezia, December 8

In the Circle of Life

In Memory of Bruno Filippi

> *The people who desire to be themselves*
> *never know where they are going.*
> ....
> *The final outcome of knowledge consists in recognizing*
> *that the soul of man is unknowable.*

Without being an imitator of rabid Papinian[13] cynicism or a super-ficial and perfumed "voluptuary" like Guido Da Verona; without feeling the ironic skepticism and the sorrowful bitterness of Mario Mariani on my lips; I feel and affirm that life cannot be at all wor-thy of the name if we do not live it as Artists, as Rebels, as Heroes.

Schopenhauer, in his powerful and frightful volumes of meta-physics, is anxious to show us that Life is sad and that for this rea-son it isn't worth the trouble of living it. But the art drawn from the most profound and lyrical human sorrow throbs to exalt the heroic Beauty that in the divinatory exaltation of symbol is trans-figured by creative joy that shows us savage purity, that sheds light on the loving spirit, that teaches us to live Life madly. If politics, socialism, christianity, humanism, logic, coherence, right, duty, just and unjust, good and evil, truth and justice, are already boring, vacuous, and slumbering things, phantoms that have grown dim and vanished in the anthropocentric sun of the unique negator; parodies of a dying civilization that inspires nausea, repugnance, and contempt in us; Art teaches us the great love of Life. We have the need to love it "up to the annihilation of being". Sorrow and Anguish are the pure fountain of pulsating Beauty for Art. It is in

---

13   Papini was an old Italian author, apparently known for his cynicism.

the sulfurous chasms of Sorrow that Art lays its luminous roots in order to be able to fling the verdant happiness of its branches high among the mysterious conflicts of the winds, in the dance of Sun and Light where dreams, hope, and Beauty are founded on a tragic song of happiness and Greatness.

Yes! Every snow-covered peak that sings polyphonic symphonies of music and poetry, of love and beauty, on high amidst the ethereal purity of light and the golden caresses of the Sun, still rises from a dark abyss. Thus is Life! Sorrow is our creative abyss, Joy and Happiness our mighty dream!

Even if sorrow does not make us better, "I think"—says Nietzsche—"that it makes us deeper." And in the mysterious depths of our being the unknowable enigma toils and hides itself. Hour by hour, moment by moment, it transmutes itself from unknown emotion to known thought, luminous and brilliant, that flashes its darting rays on virgin, purple peaks of revelatory knowledge.

And then, just as vast and glittering strings of stars wandering in the clarity of a cloudless night are reflected in the deep blue of a tranquil sea, so the happiness created by and for ourselves is reflected, smiling, in the sad sea of our sorrow; of this our sorrow that gave us Life!

We must never stop bringing our thoughts out of our sorrow and maternally giving them that within us which is of blood, of heart, of fire, of joy, of passion, of anguish, of knowledge, of destiny, of fatality.

"Life for us is to change all that we are and all that touches us into light and flame, because we cannot do otherwise." This is the circle—perhaps much too limited—of Life where we are perpetually knocked down without being able to escape except through the silent paths of Death! But Death does not frighten or terrorize us. On the contrary! We who proceed out of the Unknown of eternity and go toward the eternity of the Unknown have learned

to look upon Death like any moment of our Life. And this is our most beautiful, our most sublime mystery! This is the final word of knowledge. The unknowable!

And it is from this our unknowable singularity that the powerful and diabolical voice of our ravenous desires rises. Desires of youthful flesh eager for pleasure, the cry of the spirit panting for unlimited freedom, mad flights of the mind through the distant, unexplored unknown; howls and ferocious blasphemies of our galloping and vagabond thought colliding with the much too mysterious walls of eternity, triumphant and dionysian songs of a Life seen dimly through the delirium of a dream, a dream composed of a Whole lost and wandering in a Void. And in the void Death waits for us. This Death that is ours as Life is ours. This Death that we love!

But one should not be lowered into the grave with a heart swollen with sadness and weeping. It is necessary first to have lived in intensely as Artists, as Rebels, as Heroes, without ever having bathed in the bitter waters of repentance that flow in christian rivers. The true original and spirited sinner should not die drowning in the slimy whirlpools of a slimier remorse, but rather enveloped in the rosy blaze of the greatest sin. Before dying, we must be consumed to the last quivering spark of our luxuriant thought, having made a feast of the world and an infinite pleasure of action. Before dying, it is necessary—as Emerson said—to feel everything become familiar to us, every event useful, every day holy, every person divine. Then? "Then comes the nausea, the repugnance, the loathing," says Bruno Filippi, and then one "dares" and daring one goes with a calm and bright spirit toward the silent realm of Death where the mind is dispersed in the vast stillness of the Void and matter decomposes in order to live another type of unknown life in the atoms. But for us even Death should be a vigorous manifestation of Life, Art, and Beauty!

The Hero of Life goes toward Death accompanied by the

tragically triumphal march of dynamite and the head encircled with flowers. Yes, anyone who has desired and been able to live as Rebel and Hero wants the freedom to burn in a beautiful blaze ignited by the greatest sin so that the prelude to death is nothing but a sweet and melancholy poem kissing a red dawn where the voice of Orpheus blends with the sobs of Prometheus and the roaring, bacchic laughter of Dionysus resounds.

•

I admire Corrado Brando[14] with iconoclastic enthusiasm and atheistic religiosity even if his creator has not known how to die in time and has allowed the long rain of time to fall on his mind miraculously consuming and withering it; even though it was necessary to get drunk on the virgin and dangerous zarathustrian fountains gushing from the dizzying peaks of the merry and playful nietzschian solitude; even if the shitty little Catos[15] of that putrid Thais, of the hateful Circe called Morality, flee in horror before him. Because Corrado Brando did not glorify crime as the fat and skinny idiots claim, but—with appropriate marks of the tragic art—the efficacy and dignity of crime conceived as promethean virtue are manifested. But while I admire this vigorous creature who blossomed luxuriously through the pagan mystery of the homerically tragic art that, as a symbol of sublime heroic beauty, exalts itself above the sky of Shadow and of Night as the fatal announcement of a brilliant dawn of blood, fire, and light, I see "the anarchic individual" standing out from the grey twilight of reality, "he who obeys only his own law" in order to "open the passage with bomb explosions" and live life crying like the god of the rynerian parable: "I love you and freely desire you, oh my Necessity!" It is Bruno Filippi! Spirit has made itself Thought, Thought has made itself Flesh in order to reappear as symbol. The tragic Hero of action has made himself the artist of Life in order to transmute

---

14   A character from a novel by Gabrielle D'Annunzio.
15   The Roman orator, Cato, was known for his rigid moralism.

119

himself into the Poet of the deed, as strong and implacable as the fatality of Destiny. Like the D'Annunzian Hero. He too said with his action: "The proof of my dignity is in the invisible miracle." And just as in Corrado Brando, the intoxication of the will had accumulated in him as a Dionysian frenzy. Like the protagonist of More Than Love, he also teaches us the fury and the whirl-wind, because in him as well "the tempest raised all the forces of the soul and, tossing them about, it slammed them against a solid granite wall." Like all of the few frantic lovers of Life, he was a heroic poet of the deed who in the destruction of himself and of his Misfortunes created a tragic song to the "triumph of the imperishable will", to the cult of eternal Joy and Beauty. He offered all the corroding and luminous flames of his ardent, sorrowful, and tortured mind. He, Bruno Filippi, in the delirious impulse of his annihilation, wanted to make the most intimate and sublime Sin acknowledge Life. Then he dissolved in the Void, a luminous and wandering voice that remains for us, incessantly whispering: "Dare, dare!" And at the desperately serene cry of this symbolic twenty year old voice, it seems to us that the romantically scented pagan earth smiles at us with a lyrical and amorous smile, saying to us: "hasten destiny and come to rest in my turgid breast, swollen with fruitful seeds." Since he was a poet, Bruno Filippi heard this voice. He heard it and he answered: *Oh good earth!...I will come, I will come on the great day and you will welcome me into your arms, good, fragrant earth, and you will make the timid violets blossom on my head.* Now that Bruno Filippi has taken all the roses and thoughts germinated in the vermilion garden of his spring winds into the grave, rejoicing in strength and youth, in will and mystery, "Oh earth, take back this body and recall what was strong for your future labors." Because I see in Him as well the "necessity of the crime that burdens the resolute man elevating him at last to the titanic condition." Who was he? Where was he going?

Fools! And where have you gone? Where are you going?

He was broken while breaking the chains that you, united in a cowardly and hateful way in your manifold quality as dangerous lunatics, riveted logically and morally to his twenty year old rebel wrists in order to crush his Uniqueness, his mystery, because he was incomprehensible to you, precisely as the complicated mind of one who feels complete in himself must be. Bruno Filippi hated. But the forces of Hatred did not crush the powers of Love within Him. He immolated himself in a fruitful embrace with death because he madly loved Life. We have the need and the entitlement to say of him that which was said of the D'Annunzian hero: "That the slaves of the marketplace turn around and remember!"

Black Roses

I was lying on my purple bed—I don't know for how long—but I couldn't relax. My temples throbbed, my forehead burned as if with fever, in my brain a jumble of murky thoughts whirled, and, cursing, I vainly implored Morpheus to gather me up in his arms.

Suddenly, I saw the door of my room burst open, and gently, an *Unpredictable* entered.

I looked at her: her beautiful, deep eyes held all the secrets of the sky and all the mysteries of the seas. Her hair was long and blond. The perfume of the ripe pomegranate wafted from her mouth, awaiting the eager bite. Her rosy hands were fine and transparent, and her tiny feet were white and graceful.

Who was she? I don't know. Only she was different from the other *Unpredictable* who had already appeared to me.

She approached me smiling and sweetly ran her slender fingers through my long and unkempt hair.

My sweet one, my poor mad man, she said to me, *why do you always torment yourself so? Don't you see that your black hair is already turning white at the temples? Don't you see that your poor eyes are popping out of your head and that your facial muscles change the cast of your features in the twinge of a violent contraction? Don't you see how you are transfigured? Why this futile and endless torment of yours? Am I not the one you dreamed of, the one you waited for? Here I am!*

Ah, come, come with me, my poor man, my tender love.

You love flights, deep seas, eternal noons. I know! I know, and I understand you.

Come! Come! I have a fragrant scent, virginity and youth... I have an aura of intangible beauty, visions and dreams within me...

Come with me! I will take you far, far away, into my noble house: a white cloud wandering in the regions of the sun.

A magical wind of divine madness will emanate from the

Unknown to rock us on the waves of a radiant dream.

We will have a bed of white flowers that will never wither, and we will be happy, happy...

I will strip off my fantastic veil, lie down at your feet and play on my lyre for you, the most beautiful music that has ever been played.

I had to be pale and thoughtful at that moment!

The *Unpredictable* spoke, she spoke without pause, and her gentle words penetrated into the deepest part of my mind like sweet music, like an infinite song.

My heart was moved, and my eyes were bathed in tears.

Meanwhile, the tiny hand kept running through the forest of my hair.

My poor friend, she went on, *you are ill, very ill... but I will heal you, at least I hope to.*

I reached out my bony hands, damp with cold sweat, to grasp that blond head and pull it against my panting breast.

Ah! no... Not now, she told me, *when we get up there.*

●

What a tragic thing life is! What a horrendous conquest, tomorrow!

The very evening that followed the apparition was the most terrible I had ever passed through.

I left with the *Unpredictable*, and we wandered the whole night together in silence, and the whole following morning. In the afternoon, we reached the white cloud in the golden regions of the sun. The *Unpredictable* kept her promise... She removed the ruddy veil that covered her body, and naked and pale she offered herself to my greedy eyes. She loosened the curls of her blond hair and it fell on her snowy shoulders, and, squatting at my feet, she took up her lyre and sang me the most beautiful song that a human being could hear.

She sang while she looked fixedly into my gaping eyes as if she were searching there for my soul.

I was overcome, intoxicated, I kissed her savagely, brutally on her moist mouth of fragile rose.

Ah! fatal kiss...

Her face turned purple-blue, her eyes glazed over, the fire of her beautiful pupils was spent and her adorable body stiffened in my arms.

She was dead!

Had I just killed her? Had she wanted to die?

•

Now my muse is ringed in black, and my lyre plays funeral dirges. A black veil covers my emotions.

I feel that my mind would like to free itself once more beyond the borders of sorrow in search of the paths that lavish summer quilts with herbs and flowers; but *Fate*, against which man powerlessly roars and represses his rage, has mortally wounded her. Then the flowers—the beautiful

white flowers—withered for her and the clouds dispersed— the beautiful house of dreams—and clasping the corpse of the *Unpredictable*, I fell into the abyss.

A funeral march echoed inside me. Perhaps, tomorrow, I too will be dead.

Now I can no longer laugh at anything or anyone; I am alone with my sorrow. I believe that I am a flower born in the field of death, because I feel within myself the deadly and anguished moan of all the deceased.

Yes, I still feel the warm kiss of the sun and the caresses of the wind in my hair, but the illness—my real illness—comes from roots that still cling to the land in which I was born.

Others—those like me—are already dead or will die tomorrow, but she who should not have died is now dead.

And my *illness* is such that now I see the whole face of reality.

Unsatisfied, therefore, with the world of men, I develop the desire for a life that I have not lived and that perhaps no one could live. My forehead is ringed with large black roses: the roses of death. Iconoclasts, laugh, a funeral passes.

Nichilismo, vol.I, no.11, Milan, September 10

Spiritual Perversity

A spasm... A palpitation...

The Dawn rises from the brown bed of shadow and unties her blond braids in the laughing green morning.

Beautiful Dawn!

May she rain golden light on the white buds of the mysterious morning...

A morning of Life and Death, of love and perversity...

Yesterday evening when dusk fell and the vagabond spirits left the earth of Death to enter through paths of Silence and meditate on the luminous mysterious of the night, I created from Nothing the perverse object of my purest Love.

Now I have killed the Woman I created.

And I killed her because I loved her too much...

Her corpse lies at my feet, hideously twisted, with an everlasting red wound in her snow-white breast, opened like an eternal flower of blood.

On her purple-blue lips, a violent contraction is stamped like sarcasm and the pang that lashes out and curses... She is naked and pale.

Before long, the sun will dress her again in the moist purplish cloak of gold.

I will bend over this hidden meadow, I will make a green chalice with the poisonous leaves of bitter herbs, and I will make holy Communion with the purity of silver dewdrops.

When the sun has scattered the last traces of my baleful crime, I will play the litanies of Flowers and Death on the violin of sorrow.

2

The Night has returned.

That terrible black Night, populated by Ghosts...

Are they the phantoms of fear? Are they the shadows of remorse? Are they macabre dances of unknown truths?

O Light, why don't you set me ablaze? O Shadow, why don't you envelope me?

3

I am—like a reptile—crouching in the thorny hedge that surrounds the edge of the meadow. A toad and a serpent are my only companions.

A little ways away from me, a strange, solitary night bird sings a desperate song about the reasons for Laughter and Weeping.

But in these extreme expressions it sighs: FUTILITY!

But I can't see this very strange bird. The night is too deep... But I hear it!

Ah! what tragic voices one hears, never silent... But what does all this matter?

In the sky's blue vault, myriads of stars dance merrily...

And so? And so what does it matter if here, a short distance from me, Crime dances with Remorse, and Love is embraced by Death? Aren't the herbs of this meadow poisonous and bitter? Isn't this the Valley where the ancient immortal Gods were born to live, enjoy, and love in *perversity* and *sin*?

Then they joined the fated fishermen and raised their mortal rods.

This is why they are cursed...

4

I hear the somber roar of two distinct sounds.

The weeping of Life and the laughter of Death. How eloquent they are!...

But why does Life weep? Why does Death laugh?

5

I tried to open my eyes wide in the sun, and it blinded me.

Now I am blind. Blind and cursed...

I have nothing but darkness and silence within.

I no longer have friends or lovers. I am alone.

The kingdom of Shadow and Death is my kingdom.

I howl desperately, but in vain. My unrecognized cry is dispersed in the endless desert. It roars, it thunders, but the only response is a mournful echo.

An anguished and heart-rending echo.

6

Now I am the terrible Sinner riding the furious Centaur of Evil. I am the bridegroom of Eternity who laid himself down on a vast wave of darkness; I wager beakers of blood against the kisses of the dangerous children of Mystery.

My hands are impure because all that they have touched is impure, but in the luminous realm of my mind, flowers of the greatest purity and of an impeccable beauty have taken root.

...

A deep-sea diver, I have gone down into the deepest and most fearful chasms of the sea to rob it of its most secret treasures.

An eagle, I have soared to the highest flights of infinite space to rob it of the strangest, most ethereal mysteries.

A reptile, I have crawled on the moist earth to suck from the breasts of its infinite sweetness, the most bitter poisons.

Now I am the reckless maniacal swimmer lost in the murky waves of Life. I am the wayfarer, blaspheming and laughing, who wanders in a desert world where only the satanic howl of FUTILITY thunders.

And this is why I can heroically call myself—along with being a poet—"a truly, deeply unhappy individual."

I know I am a luminous point that goes uselessly through the gloomy futility of all things.

And it is this, my conscious desperation, this my awareness of the futility of *being*, that makes me deeply love Life.

But don't you see, my friends, that my futile joy merges into your futile sorrow, so that later both will merge into the futility of Death?

Nichilismo, vol.I, no.7, Milan, July 6

De Profundis and Germinal!

On the twilight streets of our dying age, a coffin passes.

It is the classic funeral of the old romanticsentimental art killed by the violent cerebral art of

the future.

Young rebellious, innovative artists have already hammered the bright nails of their genius into the black lid of the coffin in which the corpse of the art that was lies once and for all.

De profundis, therefore, *de profundis*.

In our city as well we wait eagerly to sing the funeral dirges to those last specters of the past that like the rancid Savoy monarchy insist on trying to live beyond their time.

But, these partisans of the past—almost aware of the dark fate that inexorably weighs on the head—don't even find in their decrepit inner being the courage to fight. This they will almost certainly notice in the next competition among artists in La Spezia.

The sad and dark prophetic foreboding of these neverborn old men forewarns them that their bloodless, grotesque creations lacking any boldness of imaginative fantasy would grow pale with impotence and shame like faded old maids, born and raised ignorant, would tremble with impotence and flush with rage finding themselves at a voluptuous, bacchanalian feast among beautiful and precocious, free and unprejudiced adolescents.

But their flight, their absenteeism, their desertion will be of no use in saving them from the fatal end marked as their destiny.

If they intervened, they would be implacably, inexorably, indisputably defeated, defeated like a dark bit of shade under a warm, golden afternoon sun shower.

If they don't intervene, their end will be even more shameful and humiliating.

De profundis! I repeat: *De profundis*! *De profundis* and

Germinal!

Make way for the impetuous, brilliant, and creative boldness of the young rebel children of the future! Glory to the coming future; forgetting the past that is left behind!

Our young artists are the ravishers of dawns and mysteries.

They are the strong and certain impregnaters of what is, and the parents of what is to come. They're not to blame if past generations didn't know decisive boldness.

But the dead are dead, and the dying will be helped to disappear.

Germinal! Germinal!

Our young people are the warm and powerful, antisentimental noontime of the future. They are the mad and reckless lovers of the strength that dares and desires; of the greatest creative strength that encloses thought within itself.

They are violent cerebralists, riding the most diabolical and raging steeds of their wise madness.

Glory then to the bold legion.

Germinal!

La testa di Ferro (The Iron Head), Fiume, no.40, p. 3, December 12

My Iconoclastic Individualism

I have left the life of the plain forever.
—Ibsen

Even the purest springs of Life and Thought that gush fresh and laughing among the rocks of the highest mountains to quench the thirst of Nature's chosen ones,

when discovered by the demagogic shepherds of the hybrid bourgeois and proletarian flocks, quickly become fetid, filthy, slimy pools. Now it is individualism's turn! From the vulgar scab to the idiotic and repulsive cop, from the miserable sell-out to the despicable spy, from the cowardly slave afraid to fight to the repugnant and tyrannical authority, all speak of individualism.

It is in fashion!

Scrawny pseudo-intellectuals of tubercular liberal conservatism, like the chronic democratic syphilitics, and even the eunuchs of socialism and the anemics of communism, all speak and pose as Individualists!

I understand that since Individualism is neither a school nor a party, it cannot be "unique", but it is truer still that Unique ones are individualists. And I leap as a unique one onto the battlefield, draw my sword and defend my personal ideas as an extreme individualist, as an indisputable Unique one, since we can be as skeptical and indifferent, ironic and sardonic as we desire and are able to be. But when we are condemned to hear socialists more or less theorizing in order to impudently and ignorantly state that there is no incompatibility between Individualist and collectivist ideas, when we hear someone stupidly try to make a titanic poet of heroic strength, a dominator of human, moral, and divine phantoms, who quivers and throbs, rejoices, and expands himself beyond the good and evil of Church and State, Peoples, and Humanity, in the strange flickering of a new blaze of unacknowledged love, like

132

Zarathustra's lyrical creator, pass as a poor and vulgar prophet of socialism, when we hear someone try to make an invincible and unsurpassable iconoclast like Max Stirner out to be some tool for the use of frantic proponents of communism, then we may certainly have an ironic smirk on our lips. But then it is necessary to resolutely rise up to defend ourselves and to attack, since anyone who feels that he is truly individualist in principle, means, and ends cannot tolerate being at all confused with the unconscious mobs of a morbid, bleating flock.

2

Individualism, as I feel, understand and mean it, has neither socialism, nor communism, nor humanity for an end. Individualism is its own end. Minds atrophied by Spencer's positivism still go on believing that they are individualists without noticing that their venerated teacher is the ultimate anti-individualist, since he is nothing more than a radical monist, and, as such, the passionate lover of unity and the sworn enemy of particularity. Like all more or less monistic scientists and philosophers, he denies all distinctions, all differences. And he sacrifices reality to affirm illusion. He strives to show reality as illusion and illusion as reality. Since he isn't able to understand the varied, the particular, he sacrifices the one or the other on the altar of the universal. Sure, he fights the state in the name of the individual, but like every sociologist in this world, he comes back to sacrifice under the tyranny of another free and perfect society, since it is true that he fights against the state, but he fights against it only because the state as it is doesn't function as he would like.

But not because he has understood the anti-collectivist, anti-social singularities capable of higher activities of the spirit, of emotion, and of heroic and uninhibited strength. He hates the state, but does not penetrate or understand the mysterious, aristocratic, vagabond, rebel individual!

And from this point of view, I don't know why that flabby charlatan, that failed anthropologist, bloated more and more with the sociology of Darwin, Comte, Spencer, and Marx, who has spread filth over the giants of Art and Thought like Nietzsche, Stirner, Ibsen, Wilde, Zola, Huysman, Verlaine, Mallarmé, etc, that charlatan called Max Nordau; I repeat, I cannot explain to myself why he hasn't also been called an Individualist... since, like Spencer, Nordau also fights the state...

3

Giovanni Papini said this about Spencer: *As a scientist, he bowed before facts, as a metaphysician, before the unknowable, as moralist, before the immutable fact of natural laws. His philosophy is made up of fear, ignorance and obedience: great virtues in the presence of Christ, but tremendous vices for one who wants the supremacy of the individual. He was neither more nor less than a counterfeiter of individualism.* And though I am not at all a Papinian, in this case I am in complete agreement with him.

4

E. Zoccoli is an intellectual of the greatest range with a deep knowledge of anarchist thought, but he declares himself to be a pathetic, moral bourgeois. In his colossal study, *Anarchy*, after railing—though calmly and with some reason—against the greatest agitators of anarchist thought, from Stirner to Tucker, Proudhon to Bakunin, he feels sorry for Kropotkin because he finds that this anarchist was not able to develop a new rigorously scientific and sociological anarchism as he allowed himself to call all the mad delinquents of extreme anarchism, or Individualism, back to the sane currents of a viscous positivistic, scientifically materialist and humanist, semi-Spencerian system, since this famous science is what finally discovered the nullity of the individual "before the limitless immensity...". And for the positivist, humanist, communist, scientific Kropotkin it also seems that man is "a small being with ridiculous pretenses" and amen! Anyone

who concentrates on sociology can't be anything but a scientist of collectivity who forgets the individual in order to seek Humanity and raise the Imperial Throne at whose feet the I must renounce itself and kneel down with deep emotion.

And when all anarchists have this sublime concept of life, E. Zoccoli will also be happy and content, since by taking on the seraphic pose of a prophet who tells men: "I have come to offer you the possibility of a new life!", he turns to us and says: "May anarchists return to (legal) right and may right expect them, quick to extend its safeguards to them as well..." But what is right?

We say with Stirner:

"Right is the *spirit of society*. If Society has a will, this will is simply Right: Society exists only through Right. But as it endures only exercising a *sovereignty* over individuals right is its **sovereign will**. Aristotle says justice is the fruit of *society*."

But "all existing right is—*alien right*; some one makes me out to be right, 'does right by me'. But should I therefore be in the right if all the world made me out so? And yet what else is the right that I obtain in the state, in society, but a right of those *alien* to me? When a blockhead makes me out in the right, I grow distrustful of my rightness; I don't like to receive it from him. But, even when a wise man makes me out in the right, I nevertheless am not in the right on that account. Whether *I* am in the right is completely independent of the fool's making out and the wise man's". Now we add to this definition of the Right that this wild, invincible German gave us, the famous aphorism of Protagoras: "The man is the measure of all things", and then we can go to war against all external right, all external justice, since "justice is the fruit of society".

I know! I know and understand: my ideas—which are not new—might wound the overly sensitive hearts of modern humanists, who proliferate in great abundance among subversives, and of romantic dreamers of a radiant, redeemed, and perfect humanity, dancing in an enchanted realm of general, collective happiness to the music of a magic flute of endless peace and universal brotherhood. But anyone who chases phantoms wanders far from the truth, and then it is known that the first to be burnt in the flames of my corroding thought was my inner being, my true self! Now within the burning blaze of my Ideas, I also become a flame, and I burn, I scorch, I corrode...

Only those who enjoy contemplating seething volcanoes that launch sinister, exploding lava from their fiery

wombs toward the stars, later letting them fall into the Void or among Dead Cities of cowardly men, my carrion brothers, making them run in frantic flight out from their moldy

wall-papered shacks, hellholes of rancid, old ideals, should approach me.

I think, I know, that as long as there are men, there will be societies, since this putrid civilization with its industries and mechanical progress has already brought us to the point

where it is not even possible to turn back to the enviable age of the caves and divine mates who raised and defended those born of their free and instinctive love like tawny, catlike Lionesses, inhabiting magnificent, fragrant, green and wild forests. But still I know and I think with equal certainty that every form of society—precisely because it is a society—will, for its own good, want to humiliate the individual. Even communism that—as its theorists tell us—is the most humanly perfect form of society would only be able to recognize one of its more or less active, more or less esteemed members in me. I can never be as worthy through communism as I will be as myself, fully my own, as a Unique one and, therefore, incomprehensible to the collectivity. But that within me which is most incomprehensible, most mysterious and enigmatic to the collectivity is precisely my most precious treasure, my dearest good, since it is my deepest intimacy which I alone can explain and love, since I alone understand it.

It would be enough, for example, if I said to communism: "it is to do nothing that the elect exist" as Oscar Wilde said, to see me driven out from the holy supper of the new Gods like a leprous Siberian! And yet one who had the urgent need to live his life in the highly and sublimely intellectual and spiritual atmosphere of Thought and contemplation could not give anything materially or morally useful and good to the community, because what he could give would be incomprehensible, and therefore noxious and unacceptable, since he could only give a strange doctrine supporting the joy of living in contemplative laziness. But in a communist society—as in any other society, where it would be even worse—such a doctrine could have the effect of corruption among the phalanx of those that must produce for collective and social maintenance and balance. No! Every form of society is the product of the majority. For great Geniuses and for great lawbreakers, there is no place within the triumphant mediocrity that dominates and commands.

6

Someone will raise the objection to me that in this vermillion Dawn, this noble eve of armies and war, where the vibrant and fateful notes of the great twilight of the old Gods already echo resoundingly, while on the horizon, the golden rays of a smiling future are already rising, it is not good to bring certain intimate and delinquent thoughts into the light of the sun. It is an old and stupid story! I am twenty-eight years old, for fifteen years I have been active in the libertarian camp and I live anarchistically, and I am told the same things, the very same things all the time:

"For the love of harmony..."

"For the love of getting the word out..."

"For the next redemptive Social Revolution..." "For..." but why go on!

Enough! I cannot remain silent!

If I were to keep a still unpublished manuscript locked up in my drawer, the manuscript of a most beautiful work that would give the reader thrills of unknown pleasure and would uncover unknown worlds; if I were certain that men would grow pale with fear over these pages, and then slowly wander through deserted pathways with eyes fiercely dilated in the void, and later would cynically seek death when madness didn't run to meet them with its sinister laughter like the roaring of winds and its grim drumming of invisible fingers on their devastated brains; if I were certain that women would smile obscenely and lie down with skirts lifted on the edge of footpaths, awaiting any male, and that males would suddenly throw themselves upon them lacerating vulva and throat with their teeth; if intoxicated, hungry mobs were to chase down the few elusive men with knives and there was death between being and being perpetuating their deep hatred; if the peace of an hour, tranquility of the spirit, love, loyalty, friendship would have to disappear from the face of the earth, and turbulence, restlessness, hatred, deception, hostility, madness, darkness and death would have to reign in their place forever; if a most beautiful book that I wrote, still unpublished and locked in my drawer, would have to do all this, I would publish that book and have no peace until it was published.

So Persio Falchi wrote in *Forca* a couple of years ago to express his concept of the Freedom of Art, and so I repeat now in *Iconoclasta!* to express my conception of Freedom of Thought.

It is an absolute and urgent need of mine to launch into the darkness the stormy and sinister light of my thoughts and the incredulous and mocking sneer of my rare ideas that want to freely wander, proud and magnificent, displaying their vigorous and uninhibited nakedness, going through the world in search of virile embraces. No one could be more revolutionary than I am, but this is precisely

why I want to throw the corroding mercury of my thoughts into the midst of the senile impotence of the eunuchs of Human Thought. One cannot be half a revolutionary and one cannot half-think. It is necessary to be like Ibsen, revolutionary in the most complete and radical sense of the word. And I feel that I am such!

7

History, materialism, monism, positivism, and all the other isms of this world are old and rusty swords which are of no use to me and don't concern me. My principle is life and my end is death. I want to live my life intensely so that I can embrace my death tragically.

You are waiting for the revolution! Very well! My own began a long time ago! When you are ready—God, what an endless wait!—it won't nauseate me to go along the road awhile with you!

But when you stop, I will continue on my mad and triumphant march toward the great and sublime conquest of Nothing!

Every society you build will have its fringes, and on the fringes of every society, heroic and restless vagabonds will wander, with their wild and virgin thoughts, only able to live by preparing ever new and terrible outbreaks of rebellion!

I shall be among them!

And after me, as before me, there will always be those who tell human beings:

"So turn to yourselves rather than to your gods or idols: discover what is hidden within you, bring it to the light; reveal yourself!"

Because everyone who searches his inner being and draws out what is mysteriously hidden there, is a shadow eclipsing every form of Society that exists beneath the rays of the Sun!

All societies tremble when the scornful aristocracy of Vagabonds, Unique ones, Unapproachable ones, rulers over the ideal, and Conquerors of Nothing advance without inhibitions. So, come on, Iconoclasts, forward!

"Already the foreboding sky grows dark and silent!"

Arcola, January

I Am Also a Nihilist

I am an individualist because I am an anarchist; and I am an anarchist because I am a nihilist. But I also understand nihilism in my own way...

I don't care whether it is Nordic or Oriental, nor whether or not it has a historical, political, practical tradition, or a theoretical, philosophical, spiritual, intellectual one. I call myself a nihilist because I know that nihilism means negation.

Negation of every society, of every cult, of every rule and of every religion. But I don't yearn for Nirvana, any more than I long for Schopenhauer's desperate and powerless pessimism, which is a worse thing than the violent renunciation of life itself. Mine is an enthusiastic and dionysian pessimism, like a flame that sets my vital exuberance ablaze, that mocks at any theoretical, scientific, or moral prison.

And if I call myself an individualist anarchist, an iconoclast, and a nihilist, it is precisely because I believe that in these adjectives there is the highest and most complete expression of my willful and reckless individuality that, like an overflowing river, wants to expand, impetuously sweeping away dikes and hedges, until it crashes into a granite boulder, shattering and breaking up in its turn. I do not renounce life.

I exalt and sing it.

2

Anyone who renounces life because he feels that it is nothing but pain and sorrow and doesn't find in himself the heroic courage to kill himself is—in my opinion—a grotesque poser and a helpless person; just as one is a pitifully inferior being if he believes that the sacred tree of happiness is a twisted plant on which all apes will be able to scramble in the more or less near future, and that then the shadow of pain will be driven away by the phosphorescent fireworks of the true Good...

3

Life—for me—is neither good nor bad, neither a theory nor an idea. Life is a reality, and the reality of life is war. For one who is a born warrior, life is a fountain of joy, for others it is only a fountain of humiliation and sorrow. I no longer demand carefree joy from life. It couldn't give it to me, and I would no longer know what to do with it now that my adolescence is past...

Instead I demand that it give me the perverse joy of battle that gives me the sorrowful spasms of defeat and the voluptuous thrills of victory.

Defeated in the mud or victorious in the sun, I sing life and I love it!

There is no rest for my rebel spirit except in war, just as there is no greater happiness for my vagabond, negating mind than the uninhibited affirmation of my capacity to life and to rejoice. My every defeat serves me only as symphonic prelude to a new victory.

4

From the day that I came into the light—through a chance coincidence that I don't care to go into right now—I carried my own Good and my own Bad with me.

Meaning: my joy and my sorrow, still in embryo. Both advanced with me along the road of time. The more intensely I felt joy, the more deeply I understood sorrow. You can't suppress the one without suppressing the other.

Now I have smashed down the door and revealed the Sphinx's

riddle. Joy and sorrow are only two liquors with which life merrily gets drunk. Therefore, it is not true that life is a squalid and frightening desert where flowers no longer blossom nor vermilion fruits ripen.

And even the mightiest of all sorrows, the one that drives a strong man toward the conscious and tragic shattering of his own individuality, is only a vigorous manifestation of art and beauty.

And it returns again to the universal human current with the dazzling rays of crime that breaks up and sweeps away all the crystallized reality of the circumscribed world of the many in order to rise toward the ultimate ideal flame and disperse in the endless fire of the new.

5

The revolt of the free one against sorrow is only the intimate, passionate desire for a more intense and greater joy. But the greatest joy can only show itself to him in the mirror of the deepest sorrow, merging with it later in a vast barbaric embrace. And from this vast and fruitful embrace the higher smile of the strong one springs, as, in the midst of conflict, he sings the most thundering hymn to life.

A hymn woven from contempt and scorn, from will and might. A hymn that vibrates and throbs in the light of the sun as it shines on tombs, a hymn that revives the nothing and fills it with sound.

6

Over the Socrates' slave spirit that stoically accepts death and Diogenes' free spirit that cynically accepts life, rises the triumphal rainbow on which the sacrilegious crusher of new phantoms, the radical destroyer of every moral world, dances. It is the free one who dances on high amidst the magnificent phosphorescence of the sun.

And when huge clouds of gloomy darkness rise from swampy chasms to hinder his view of the light and block his path, he opens the way with shots from his Browning[16] or stops their course with the flame of his domineering fantasy, forcing them to submit as humble slaves at his feet.

But only the one who knows and practices the iconoclastic fury of destruction can possess the joy born of freedom, of that unique freedom fertilized by sorrow. I rise up against the reality of the outer world for the triumph of the reality of my inner world.

I reject society for the triumph of the I. I reject the stability of every rule, every custom, every morality, for the affirmation of every willful instinct, all free emotionality, every passion, and every fantasy. I mock at every duty and every right so I can sing free will.

I scorn the future to suffer and enjoy my good and my bad in the present. I despise humanity because it is not my humanity. I hate tyrants and I detest slaves. I don't want and I don't grant solidarity, because I am convinced that it is a new chain, and because I believe with Ibsen that the one who is most alone is strongest.

This is my Nihilism. Life, for me, is nothing but a heroic poem of joy and perversity written with the bleeding hands of sorrow and pain or a tragic dream of art and beauty!

Nichilismo, Year I no.4, Milan, May 21

---

16   A type of pistol popular among anarchists of the time.

My Maxims

From the notebook of my intimate thoughts:

GOD: The product of sick fantasies. Inhabitant of senile and impotent brains. Companion and comforter of rancid spirits born to slavery. Cocaine for hysterics. A pill for constipated minds closed to knowledge. Marxism for the faint of heart.

HUMANITY: An abstract word with a negative connotation, long on force, short on truth. An obscene mask painted on the foul and filthy face of the most vulgar wise ass for the purpose of dominating the crudely sentimental, vulgar herd of idiots and imbeciles.

FATHERLAND: Intellectual life imprisonment for the semi-intelligent, a pigsty of imbecility. A Circe who transforms her adoring fans into dogs and pigs.

A whore for her master, a pimp of the foreigner. She eats her own children, slanders her own parents and mocks her own heroes.

FAMILY: The denial of Love, Life and Liberty.

SOCIALISM: Discipline, discipline; obedience, obedience; slavery and ignorance, pregnant with authority.

Socialism is a bourgeois body grotesquely fattened by a vulgar christian creature.

It is a medley of fetishism, sectarianism and cowardice.

ORGANIZATIONS, LEGISLATIVE BODIES, AND UNIONS: Churches for the powerless. Pawnshops for skinflints and trash. Many join to live parasitically off the backs of their card-carrying simpleton colleagues. Some join to become spies. Others, the most sincere, believe me—and poor naïve devils—join to end up in jail where they can observe the shameful cowardice of all the rest. The greatest part of the mass to pay, yawn and wait.

SOLIDARITY: The macabre altar on which actors of every sort display their priestly qualities by ably reciting their mass. The beneficiaries pay nothing less than complete humiliation.

FRIENDSHIP: Fortunate are those who have drunk from its chalice without having their spirit offended and their mind poisoned. If any such person exists, I warmly urge him to send me his photograph. I'm almost certain I will look upon the face of an idiot.

LOVE: Deception of the flesh and damage to the spirit. Disease of the soul, atrophy of the brain, fainting of the heart, corruption of the senses, poetic lies on which I get ferociously drunk two or three times a day so that I can consume this precious but oh so stupid life more quickly. And yet I would prefer to die of Love. It's the only scoundrel, after Judas, that can still kill with a kiss.

MAN: A filthy paste of servitude and tyranny, fetishism and fear, vanity and ignorance.

The greatest offence one could commit against an ass is to call it a man.

WOMAN: The most brutal of all enslaved beasts. The greatest victim that crawls on the earth. But the most to blame—after man and dog, deserving of all her woes. I'd be truly curious to know what she thinks of me when I kiss her.

Oh, cynical prostitute, daring female expropriator, you raise yourself above the putridity in which the world is immersed and you cause it to grow pale under the perverse light of your great deep eyes.

You are the most beautiful star that the sun now kisses. You are of another breed. And your mind is a song, your life a dream.

You unhinge the world, oh free prostitute, oh daring female expropriator.

I will sing for you. The rest is mud.

Iconoclasta!, no.12, Pistoia, October 15, 1920

Parabola

Yes, I am a many-sided being and a complicated reality!

It is only in the mirror of past memories and in dreams of the future that I can penetrate, contemplate, and comprehend the real and deep essence of this enigmatic and mysterious being of mine.

Humans, oh my dear lost and renegade brothers and sisters, in truth I say to you that I am an egoistic giver; but to you I can only offer the shadow of myself. If it interests you to find me, I live behind this shadow. I inhabit the laughing house of the most joyous sorrow. But tell me, oh my brothers and sisters, tell me, my friends: which of you was always able to resist the eye of the tempting Demon, the eye of the sinning Serpent?

Brothers and sisters, I am Evil, the Great, the True, the Magnificent Evil!

Look out for my shadow. I live behind her very sweetly cradled by the invisible arms of my ethereal lover, of my divine and hellish madness. (I have called her this because she is born from a mad embrace between Dream and Imagination, between Matter and the Idea that happened in forests sacred to Sorrow). But she is not, like Death, a lover of pale and odorous flesh. O brothers and sisters, no! Your lovers of flesh have lost you. Mine of spirit and light have exalted, transfigured, purified, and redeemed me...

Oh Shadow! Oh my Shadow, save me now from the cynical look of my rival brothers and sisters, so that Evil and Madness, in a tight embrace, dance now in the deepest, most luminous abyss of this being of mine.

Oh, how sublime is the divine mystery of MADNESS!

Now I contemplate the Sacred Arc of the eternal fire. On this—with hair undone—I see life—my life—rising up naked with a bacchic Thyrsus tight in hand adorned with bunches of blond and red grapes. Now I walk fantastically with bare, winged feet on the free and laughing paths of the spirit illuminated by a sparkling, bloody dawn. And I run over there, far away, toward the blistering noontime rays of

the ultimate sun to "cheerfully decay in its kiss." This is what the solitary vagabonds come to.

The Madmen, the Poets, the Heroes.

Oh my ultimate and true friends, come, it is time, it is time!

Don't you see over there, in the distance, that pure City of the whitest snow?

Oh friends, friends, be strong because tragedy draws near...

Quickly watch the pure, white city melt under the scorching power of the Sun.

Ah, the Sun, the Sun! The ultimate Fire, the ultimate Force, the ultimate Beauty, the ultimate majestic and sacrilegious Power...

But you, oh my Madness, why ever therefore do you sneer so mockingly?

Ah, I understand, I understand...

Your smile is a jeer. Perhaps your ultimate most powerful jeer?! Yes, perhaps...

1921

In the Realm of Phantoms

written under the pseudonym Brunetta the Incendiary

> *Only Beauty and Force exist, but for balance,*
> *louts and weaklings invent Justice.*
> —Raffaele Valente

I thought it was a frightning dream and instead it was a bloody reality. I am besieged and suppressed in a double thought it was a frightening dream and instead it is a circle of the mad and the possessed.

The world is a pestilent, filthy, slimy church where everyone has an idol to worship as a fetish and an altar on which to sacrifice themselves. Even those who lit the iconoclastic pyre to burn down the cross on which the god-man was nailed, have not yet understood life's cry or freedom's howl. After Jesus Christ, from the depths of his legend, spat the bloodiest insult in man's face, inciting him to deny himself so that he could approach god, the French Revolution came—savage irony—making the very same appeal by proclaiming the "rights of man."

For Christ and the French Revolution, man is incomplete.

Christ's cross symbolizes the POSSIBILITY of becoming MAN; the "rights of man" symbolize the same thing.

For the former, it is necessary to become divine to reach perfection, and for the latter, it is necessary to become human.

But both agree in proclaiming the incompleteness of the human-individual, the actual I, affirming that only through the realization of the ideal can man achieve the magic peaks of perfection.

Christ tells you: if you will patiently climb bleak Calvary and be nailed to the cross, becoming MY image, I, the god-man, you will be the perfect human creature worthy to sit on my Father's right hand in the kingdom of heaven.

And the French Revolution tells you: I have proclaimed the

rights of man. If you devoutly enter the cloister of human social justice to sublimate and humanize yourself through the moral canons of social life, you will be a citizen and I will give you your rights, proclaiming you a man. But anyone who'd dare to throw the cross—where the god-man hung, and the tablets—where the rights of man are ominously incised, into the flames, to then set the focal axis of their life on the virgin, granite boulder of free force, would be an impious and wicked person against whom the bloody jaws of two sinister phantoms would turn: the jaws of the divine and of the human.

To the right, the sulfurous and everlasting flames of hell that punish SIN, and to the left, the hollow creaking of the guillotine that condemns CRIME.

The cold and dispirited cowardice of human fear, sprouted from the theorization of a mystical and diseased emotion, could finally triumph over the healthy and primitive, instinctive and spirited INJUSTICE that was merely Force and Beauty, Youth and Daring. So-called progress and so-called civilization, so-called religion and the so-called ideal have locked life in a deadly circle where the most baleful phantoms have built their unctuous realm.

Now is the time to put an end to it! We need to violently break through the circle and escape. If the chimeras of divine legend have had a horrible influence on human history and if human history requires the mutilation of the instinctiveactual man to follow its course: we will rebel against it!

It isn't our fault if the most purulent drops of pus have spurted from Christ's symbolic wounds onto humanity's red light, breeding the corrupting civil rot that proclaimed the rights of man. If men want to rot away in the systematic caverns of social putrefaction, they can settle right in. We won't be the ones to free them! Rather we are the ones who love the Sun and want to abandon ourselves to the violent passion of its kiss.

***

When I look around me, I get the urge to vomit.

On one side, the scientists who I am supposed to believe so as not to be ignorant. On the other side, the moralists and philosophers, whose commandments I am supposed to accept so as not to be a brute.

Then comes the Genius that I am supposed to glorify and the Hero before whom I am to bow, moved.

Then along come the comrade and the friend, the idealist and the materialist, the atheist and the believer and an infinity horde of defined and undefined apes who want to give me their good advice and finally set me on the true path. Because—of course—the path I walk is false, as my ideas, my thoughts, my entire being are false.

I am a false man. They—poor lunatics—are all obsessed with the idea that life has called them to be priests officiating at the altar of the greatest missions, since humanity is called to the greatest destinies… These poor, pathetic beasts, scarred by sham ideals and transfigured by madness, could never understand the tragic and merry wonder of life, as they could never see that humanity is not really called to any great destiny. If they had understood any of this at all, they would have at least learned that their so-called likes actually have no desire to break their backs bridging the chasm that separates one from the other.

But I am what I am, it doesn't matter.

And the cawing of these multicolored magpies only serves to brighten up my personal and noble wisdom. Oh, apostolic apes of humanity and social progress, don't you hear something thundering above your phantoms?

Listen, listen! It is the piercing roar of my wild laughter that is rumbling overhead, in the heights!

Vertice, Arcola, April 21

The Revolt of the Unique

To comrade Carlo Molaschi with strength of mind and serenity of thought.

I don't want to dictate moral maxims to my "neighbor," or teach anyone anything... I leave this task to the missionaries of all faiths, the priests of all churches, the demagogues of all parties, the apostles of all ideas.

I only want to howl my extreme rebellion against everything that oppresses me; I only want to push far away from me everything that the religious, socialist, or libertarian priesthood wants to impose on my individuality without me having freely accepted and wanted it.

Digging into the underground of my depths, I have been able to penetrate the mystery of my "I" (emotional— spiritual—physical—instinctive); I have been able to discover my will and my power; I have been able to take possession of my "uniqueness."

The dogmatic frogs of societarianism and the gooses of the ideal croaked, but their croaking only served to fill my heart with intoxication and distill poisons in my words.

The theoretical and philosophical chattering of the ruling plebeian "wisdom" no longer moves me, just like the choreographic demonstrations of starving mobs or those of the people cheering new redeeming Jesuses no longer move me...

I have a personal truth of my own that isn't and can't be universal "truth." I am guided by an instinct, by a feeling, by a dream, that are only the triology composing the unique ideal that is my individuality. Individuality that nobody except me and my power can make strong, free, and happy!...

I don't deny to anyone the beauty of their ideas, the strength of their dream, and the truth of their thought.

I know that everyone may lock within himself precious mines

filled with unknown treasures; I know that where a human being lives there is—or can be—a world with all its lands and seas, its joys and sorrows, its sun and stars, its loves and hates.

Let each human being therefore work—if he thinks this way—at the discovery of his own I, at the realization of his own dream, at the complete integration and full development of his own individuality. Every human being who has discovered and won himself walks on his own path and follows his free course.

But let no one come to me to impose his belief, his will, his faith on me. By denying god, fatherland, authority, and law, I have achieved anarchism. By refusing to sacrifice myself on the altar of the people and of humanity, I have achieved individualism.

Now I am free...

The war that I opened against phantoms has ended with my victory. Now the cycle of a new war has opened!

The war against the brute force of society, of the people, of humanity. Against these terrible and colossal monsters that aren't ashamed to dare to act against the unique and the brutal force of their thousand monstrous arms, I "authorize" myself to defend myself with all the weapons that it is possible for me to dare to use: with all those means that I have the power and the ability to make use of. Without scruples!

Because I am one who really follows himself!

I cultivate the flowers of my garden and I quench my thirst at my own springs.

If for you my flowers are poisonous and my waters bitter, to me instead they fill the heart with a fierce joy and give me wild and heroic quivers in the flesh and spirit.

When I think of the claims of missionaries and teachers; of moralists and educators, I get the desire to laugh.

You are utterly absurd, oh lost soul. You are a poor lunatic who lives in <u>the moral (?)</u>. You are an exaggeration; you walk a false and wrong path. Your 'morale' is fierce, your principle is 'cruel'!" So, more or less, the knowing "sages" of universal happiness want to talk to me, the stammering fools of "good" and "evil." those who have discovered "truth" and buried "lies"...

Now god is dead, they say, the fatherland is destroyed, authority has collapsed. Forward, everywhere, young people, for the proletarian international, for the joy of knowing universal happiness. And anyone who won't die for this 'sacred cause' is a fierce 'egoist,' a 'wicked' person, a 'traitor'! It seems they want to say, or rather they do say, *The human being doesn't count; the idea counts; Humanity counts!*

And I, poor microscopic insect, poor powerless cell diseased with Stirner's "fierce egoism"—not to mention infected by arrogant Zarathustrian overhumania—am something less than nothing, an invisible particle that is of no use at all except as raw material put at the disposal of the great architects of the universe; except as a sacrificial beast to give in fiery slaughter to the goddess "humanity," to the god "people" or to the Sun of the future...

2

Comrade Carlo Molaschi will think: but of what use is this whole sermon of Renzo Novatore's, made as a prelude to a polemical writing dedicated to me?

Don't I also know these things?

Aren't they also old things of the Earth and the Sun?

But he will add: *The individualist current of anarchism threatened—and perhaps still threatens—to degenerate into absurdity (?). Stirner with his gospel of fierce egoism, has tried to slaughter human feeling in the individual; and the presumptuous egoism of the overhuman has led many comrades to the adoration of his own I.*

And he will continue: *But anarchist individualism should not* (pay attention to the "should not": I am the one who has emphasized it) *be either the ferocity of the Unique, nor the arrogance of Zarathustra.*

Mutual aid, solidarity, and love are necessities of life!

Let's leave aside for a moment the "fierce egoism of Stirner's Unique" that is so cruelly fierce as to affirm that he is only "hostile" to all that is "dark." Let's leave aside for now that cynical "slaughterer of human feeling" (I say liberator of human feeling) who said: "My egoism is not opposed to love, is not the enemy of sacrifice and self-denial... and not even of socialism, in short, not the enemy of actual interests, and rebels not against love, but against sacred love, not against thought, but against sacred thought, not against socialism but against sacred socialism."[17] But—as I said—let's leave aside for a moment this terrible "slaughterer of human feeling" and with him let's also leave aside that "arrogant and presumptuous Zarathustra" or, to be more precise, Friedrich Nietzsche; that cruel Friedrich Nietzsche, who is without a doubt the highest bard of humanity, and the strongest and deepest—and let's get to ourselves.

Thus, that "should not" that I noted earlier starts to mean that individualism SHOULD be what he—Carlo Molaschi—preaches!

And when he says: "Mutual aid, brotherhood, love are needs of life!" (he once said—see the magazine *Libertà*, #7, November 1, 1913: "I despise solidarity, I feel that I am a stranger to humanity"), I respond that while admitting that they are a necessity, they are not and cannot be "a reality"! I say it of universal and particular reality.

Reality is hatred, enmity, war! Carlo Molaschi will answer: it is necessary to smash this reality; once he said (see the writing of his cited above): *I have no need to believe or hope in any Paradise, or*

---

17   This is a paraphrase of this passage from *Stirner's Critics*: "Egoism, as Stirner uses it, is not opposed to love nor to thought; it is no enemy of the sweet life of love, nor of devotion and sacrifice; it is no enemy of intimate warmth, but it is also no enemy of critique, nor of socialism, nor, in short, of any actual interest. It doesn't exclude any interest. It is directed against only disinterestedness and the uninteresting; not against love, but against sacred love, not against thought, but against sacred thought, not against socialists, but against sacred socialists, etc."

to delude myself that my existence has to cooperate in making way for human progress; but that Judas comes to create the other "reality" that is necessary here! And we still accept this as well... but for hundreds of centuries, prophets have announced this new "reality," martyrs have fallen, rebels have died, heroes have gone up on the guillotine, but with each day that passes, the hatred floods more strongly over the world, the mania for authority increases frightfully in every human heart, wars multiply and the "masses," the "crowds," the "proletarians"—despite illusory appearances—become more and more weary, more and more cowardly, more and more craven.

Molaschi will say (see *"We and the Mass" in issue 9 of Nichilismo,* August 24, 1920): "We ourselves are children of the people (what a marvelous father!), we feel the very suffering of the mass"; he once said (see *Libertà* cited above): "I live among human beings who seem similar to me; but I am not like them. They are refined or dissatisfied; I am restive, attentive to the reins of the law"; and he suffers under the yoke of a habit.

But I respond: the dream of workers is not my dream. The longings of the people are not my longings, the pains of the mass are not my pains!...

I feel the sorrow of my depth and the bitterness of what is impossible to me!

A crust of black bread is enough to satisfy the mass, but my longings cannot be satisfied!

It's true that Carlo Molaschi gleefully rubs his hands and says: *The Italian Syndicalist Union is strongly influenced by our ideas, many of its spokespeople are our comrades, we have a daily paper of national importance read by more than thirty five thousand people...* He once said (see *Il Ribelle* issue 6, January 2, 1915): *Anarchists have been and are much too concerned with proselytizing. Conferences and papers on propaganda...just to convince idiots who never knew how and never will know how to "feel" any ideal to call themselves anarchists.*

—But I still laugh skeptically at these new Molaschian enthusiasms as he once laughed skeptically when he stated that "anarchists are born and not made" and that he didn't give a damn for the "future" since he was "free" having made himself the "purpose of his life."

Carlo Molaschi says (see the comment he made to Vivani's writing "I Will Be Pure," published in issue 5 of *Pagine Libertarie*): "... the human being is free in so far as he lives in harmony with nature and with his likes." He once said (quoting that "arrogant and presumptuous" "man of genius" who then had "ideas like his"): "The weak and infirm die. First principle of our love for the human being. We need rather to help them disappear."

—But I cannot live in "universal" harmony with my "likes" for the simple reason that they are not... and cannot be—for the reason that I have already outlined in the prelude of this piece of mine—my "likes."

My likes are few in the relative sense and none at all in the absolute sense. So with the few that are like me in the

"relative" sense, I remain in agreement against the multitude; in the absolute sense I remain alone—Unique—against them and the others. They become in their turn the "weak," and the "infirm," for me!

But now I seem to have wandered far enough. So let's stop!

Carlo Molaschi will smile ironically and say: *That fine devil Renzo Novatore has put out my old articles for scrutiny to show my contradictions, but by doing this he manages to do nothing other than to "show" how much ignorance he still holds in his mind. He ignores the laws... of evolution!*

Well, no, comrade Molaschi, it is not through pure and simple ignorance that I have done all this. No!

I did it for quite another reason...

I know what I wanted to note in you, you could—at least in

the reverse direction—note it in myself and in all those who are not crystallized fossils.

But I did it just to show you that it is, at least, ridiculous to state that individualism "should" be that of Tucker and not that of Stirner. "Should" be this and "should" not be that!...

As far as the negating concept of anarchism we walk together; when anarchism becomes individualist, every individuality follows his or her own path. Yes, human beings evolve!

At eighteen years of age, when experience is zero and the mind is excited by reading books very poorly understood, one can—at times—take on the menacing appearance of the overhuman; but later, when experience starts to analyze life then one evolves...

And in evolving one now denies everything that one affirmed yesterday!

And that's fine.

But no one has the "obligation" or the "duty" to follow the single path of our evolution... or devolution!...

Because someone who followed the evolution of Giovanni Papini would have ended up in church with him; one who followed Libero Tancredi ends up in interventionism and fascism; one who follows Renzo Novatore could end up one day with him in a lunatic asylum—perhaps a "libertarian communist" one. And one who would follow Carlo Molaschi might end up—how do I say it?—as Carlo Molaschi will end up!

And this is why, oh my friend, I am against that "should" which you, in my opinion, still pronounce with too much ease...

You see? If I am supposed to say something to these my "likes"— who are not my likes—especially to the young ones—I will say this to them: Beware oh young spirits! Beware of the old sirens! The old have ideas that cannot be those of youth. So seek again your cast-off selves. Discover yourselves. Don't let yourselves be violated! Old Tolstoy is a majestic, unshakable, gigantic figure. But I would pity any youth who professed the ideas of this old man!

Before coming to christianity, Papini passed through all rebellions. Then tired, exhausted, finished, he threw himself down on the bed of weakness, of impotence, of senility.

He cast himself upon the bosom of "our mother church"!

Discover yourselves, oh young ones! Dig into yourselves. In each of you there must be precious mines of unknown treasures. But if in digging into your I you find nothing, don't look for anything in anyone. The most real and precious jewels would transmute into false stones in your hands. Because "anarchists are born and not made," as comrade Molaschi once said....

3

"The anti-society perspective that tried several years ago to make inroads in the movement of anarchist ideas," Molaschi says, "has faded."

But all this that comrade Carlo Molaschi affirms is not entirely true...

It's true that with the daily paper *Umanità Nova*, the conferences, the unions, the workerism, the organizations, anarchism has ended up making itself official and becoming a party.

It's true that comrade Carlo Molaschi feels a great "joy" in finding himself in agreement with comrade Damiani; that he is "satisfied" to be in agreement with Luigi Fabbri and that he "shares" Malatesta's ideas.

It's true that Carlo Molaschi wants to make a mark, "orienting" individualism in his way!

But it's still not true that the "anti-society" current of individualism has completely faded into the heaven of anarchy.

There is still some "wild" reprobate, in the midst of so much paternal democratic domesticity, who holds the "barbaric" banner of anti-society individualism!

Yes: there is still someone...

4

First of all, we need to come to a bit of an agreement about what "anti-society" means.

I am not a misanthrope and so much the less a misogynist...

I need friends and lovers, clothes and bread. I am not an anchorite or a saint in the desert.

But there's no need to be such a thing in order to be anti-society. Being anti-society means—for me—not collaborating in the preservation of the present society nor lending one's efforts to any new social construction.

I said it once before:

Every society you build will have its fringes, and on the fringes of every society, heroic and restless vagabonds will wander, with their wild and virgin thoughts, only able to live by preparing ever new and terrible outbreaks of rebellion!

I shall be among them!

And if materialistic "needs" force me to go toward society, the "necessity" to be free sets me against it and gives birth in me to a third "need." That of doing violence to it. Without scruples!

This is my "anti-society" perspective. And if we happened to speak of so-called "progress" I could even affirm— without fear of going wrong—that the triumph and the glory of the human path are due only to the spirit that informs this anti-society principle of individualism.

5

Carlo Molaschi who has launched himself with fury against the overhuman to throw it into the sea and against Stirner's "association of egoists" to make it suffer the same end; now he proclaims with the impulse of faith B. R. Tucker's "association of the free," because—he says—"Tucker in his project of the association of the free allows that minorities, when they don't agree with majorities, can split (oh, strange miracle!...) from the association and create another one of their own."

But I bet that Carlo Molaschi knows much better than me what "might" be—or rather—what "is" hidden in that:

"when they don't agree"!

Yes: Molaschi knows!...

6

The word "Freedom" taken in itself is a negation: nothing—death!

Freedom is a propulsion towards power—it is the strength of conquest and the capacity for possession.

(I have had the capacity to free myself from that tiresome old lover of mine; because I had the capacity and the power, I have taken the liberty of gathering this new flower).

Living means doing good and bad to others. No one can live without hurting anyone....

Living means: dominating and being dominated!

With the realization of the unpleasant authoritarian communism of the socialists, the rulers would be a slimy handful of demagogues, vulgar, cunning insects; plebeian slaves in their turn of a dogma.

In realizing libertarian communism, the great majority would be the ruling Goddess. But libertarian communism (which is the dream of those who hate conflict and battle— which is youth and life—and for which they are nonetheless quick, strange a paradoxical contradiction, to make war in the name of equality and peace) would have to take extreme measures against those who want to come out, advance, rise up to a more ample affirmation of individual life.

Libertarian communism would then be forced to repress in

order to preserve itself. But its materialistic preservation would be the categorical negation of the very spirit that informs and exalts it!

And here we are finally at anarchy—I admit that one can speak of this as a social realization of human life together. "Anarchy" would thus be nothing more nor less than the triumph of the higher "type."

Radically vanished—because even the lowliest of all human beings would have had to go beyond it—the as-stupid-as-it-is-vulgar right to private property and everything that is "material good." The spiritual dominator remains— the one who is noble by nature. He will stand above the others and dominate them.

(No one, I believe, would have the false pretension of levelling ethical, aesthetic, artistic, intellectual, and spiritual values, like physical and sexual values). Because the noble one, even in Anarchy—or rather, in anarchy more than in any other form of human life together—will enjoy pleasure that others would not be able to enjoy, even if he, for love of them, wanted to renounce them. Anarchy is therefore the natural Autocracy of the noble.

A simple test that thousands of other complicated ones are equal to him there. Yesterday a young woman offerred herself— marvelous gift—to the charming and noble dominator Pietro Gori.

Today in the whirpools of misery if a stunted "papa's" boy who nature has condemned bought her! He has enjoyed with money the fruit that in Anarchy he would never have been able to enjoy. And I'm no longer able to argue that in anarchy a cobbler is the same as a genius or that a hunchback is equal to an Adonis.

We can give both the same bread, but not the same pleasures.

And if it is true that friendship and love give joy and pleasure, I would just like to ask any anarchist if he can give his old semi-idiotic doorman what, in fact, he gives to Errico Malatesta in love and friendship.

I would just like to ask a few of our free and intelligent woman comrades if she can give to any nasty, conceited, vain, ambitious "comrade" what she willingly concedes to a kind, cultivated, loving, good comrade...

I repeat: Anarchy—for me—means: Autocracy of beauty, of genius, of art, and of all those who possess the willful and selective qualities suitable for dominating and that mother nature—justly or unjustly—grants and lavishes so generously on a few, while she denies them to most, as if the latter were her bastard children!

And if the overhuman that you—oh comrade Molaschi—have thrown with implacable fury into the stormy waves of the sea, were that elect—superior—type to which I just now alluded, it's enough that he rise up again out of the waters more beautiful and stronger than before, since this race is an immortal race.

Everyone can be levelled before society (we are all equal before god!...) but the selective-individual values remain. They remain and dominate!

And for these and a thousand other reasons, in my relations with the present society, I declare myself "united" with Stirner's Unique, and in my posthumous relations with the future society of distant becoming, I feel drawn toward the Antichrist and Zarathustra transformed and purified in the sun of my thought.

Of course, I am neither Max Stirner, nor Friedrich Nietzsche. Rather, halfway, between me and them there might be a fearful depth powerfully dug out by the mystic Tolstoy, or the high and dreadful peaks illuminated by the voluptuously tormented spirit of Ibsen, as there could also be the conflagration of the pure and perverse Wildean mind!

7

Dear Molaschi, I am at the end. The polemic with you is done.

As you have seen, more than a polemic, it is a confession and a declaration.

I believe you've understood me.

I know that often the form takes hold of my hand and wraps and twists itself around the nakedness of my thought, like a beautiful and perverse female wraps herself around the virile body of the lover, almost managing to hide it from the modest eyes of most.

But this time I believe that it hasn't been like this.

I have many times, but many times I have decidedly failed...

Then the writing is dedicated to you!

And you are not one of the many!

Your eyes are certainly able to see even a bit in the night...

Even though you don't share my ideas, I am certain that you understand me.

And that is what I want! Only that...

There was a time when I understood you as flesh of my flesh, feeling my feeling. Now no longer!

And that is why my love toward you fades away among the shadows of a memory, but leaves the torches of the strongest, most sincere admiration lit.

We may have started from the same stream, but we started on the path to two different mountains. If we both reach the peaks we will stretch out our hands over the gulf since we will have conquered fate and overcome the abyss.

And then we will love each other with a different love!

Pagina Libertaria, vol.I, no.6, Milano, September 15

A Portrayal of Sorts

I don't announce or promise anything.

There are too many lying prophets who announce the possibility of a new life; and even more vulgar plebeians of the spirit who promise the world—new Jesuses—with their unredeemed blood…

Who am I? I don't know! I can't describe myself!…

I know I am a mixture of modesty and pride, wisdom and ignorance, vice and virtue, cowardice and heroism, light and gloom, logic and absurdity.

I am suspended above the abyss of unexplored depth with my eyes fixed on a distant peak that may be nothing more than an illusion.

I know there are within me sunlit and blossoming summits like fantastic summer gardens, and dark hidden caverns that will never see the light of day. I have found FRIENDS who are a bit like me because I am a bit like them, and we have agreed to build a crystalline house together on the rocks of a PEAK.

We don't for this reason believe ourselves gods.

But there are eagles and snakes who, like gods, love the virgin heights… and we are among them.

Therefore, we are animals, but animals of the peaks! Animals crouched in strange postures among the symbolic shrubs of truly free art, we will cultivate poisonous flowers of pure beauty even though the apes who live in the low social swamps hurl their powerless anathema and their hoarse, ridiculous curses toward our nest of violent loners.

I've finished my declaration, but I haven't described myself.

I know that anyone, even the most humble of mortals, has the right to make a declaration of this sort. But I also know that aside from having the right to it, the most brilliant genius must see it as an absolute DUTY.

Vertice, Arcola, April 21

Introduction to the Review Vertice

with co-editors Tintino Rasi and Giovanni Governato

We feel that we are absolutely beyond all *isms* and theories. We will finally suppress all the practices of kooks and scribblers who try to impose themselves by every means on the attention of the refined by relying on avant-garde tendencies whose ideas they have often not digested very well. We relentlessly refuse all products of purely technical virtuosity, where they don't serve to express a striking aesthetic rebellion. Dark, virgin forces, laughing ravishers of the impossible, audacious explorers of the peaks and the depths, we thunder our agonizing howl of beauty that crushes the verminous swarm of weaklings, the stinking multitude.

The Dream of My Adolescence
written under the pseudonym Sibilia Vane

May the wisdom of rotten idiots not sneer nor the idiotic chastity of decent young ladies be scandalized.

I am a precocious adolescent who, after a long journey through the phosphorescent labyrinths of the most terrifying depths, climbed back up to the peak to sing the proud and sacrilegious song of my still young and oh so free life in the sun.

Someone told me: "You will be a woman, then a wife, then a mother!..."

I answered like this, with a question: What do woman, wife, and mother mean? I won't tell you what they said in response. I only know that when I think about it, I laugh, yes, I still laugh. Love understood as a mission!? The woman as wife and mother? No, no, no! I will not be a wife; I will not be a mother! My revolt cannot stop halfway or make mistakes. My revolt even casts its darts—beyond the family—against nature. I don't want to be a wife; I don't want to be a mother.

No, no, no!

•

Yesterday, I stripped naked before the mirror and looked at myself for a long time. I saw my body of flesh wrapped in a shadow of light that quivered slightly. I don't quite know why, but I adored myself....

The turgid breasts rose proudly from the chest, a treasure of creamy whiteness. My smooth, round belly gave me the impression that it was something that had been shaped from the finest ivory by the miraculous hands of a godlike artist. I had loosened the blonde ringlets of my hair over the curved smoothness of my shoulders and lightly circled my moist-lidded eyes with violet and black. The down that crowned the lower concavity of my belly looked like a golden wing on the sacred spine of heavenly angels.

My red mouth appeared to be a ripe pomegranate opened to the yellow caress of the sun.

I approached the mirror and voluptuously kissed my reflected lips.

I don't know if I have ever in my life desired anything with more intensity than, yesterday evening, when I desired to be a man so that I myself could lay the white virgin body, which the mystery in the clear mirror had shown me, down on the bed.

But the idea of intercourse brought forth another idea in me. Every cause has an effect.

I lay down on the bed. My temples throbbed. The blood boiled in my veins. Perhaps I was delirious...

I know that I had my eyes closed and only saw darkness. But amidst the darkness I saw another mirror. The mirror of the imagination, which showed reality. I looked at myself. I saw my fine, round, varnished belly fearfully swollen, with a symmetrical black-yellow line that gave me the clammy impression of a small grass snake stretched out on a sack full of bulky, withered grass.

Then, I also saw my superb, white breasts gone flabby and shriveled... I was a mother!

A hateful brat greedily sucked my blood , spoiled my youth, mercilessly destroyed my divine beauty that I had hoped would be immortal.

Yesterday evening's desire has passed, but the nightmare remains.

Mother... What does it all mean? Giving children to the species, more slaves to society, more derelicts to sorrow.

... Mother... Wife....

Are these then the aims of love?

Ah, the old sorcery of morality, the old lies of this old humanity.

No, I will never be anyone's wife; I will never give any children to the species. Never!

Life is pain. Humanity is a lie. Anyone who accepts

perpetuating the species is an enemy of pure beauty.

Humanity is a race that must FADE AWAY!

Individualism must kill society, pleasure must strangle pain. Let weeping and pain die, drowned in a final orgy of joy. Give yourself to the mad joy of living, you who love life, you who love the end.

Why should the future matter? What does the species matter to you?

Come on, you who have discovered yourselves, let's make the world a feast. Let's make life a twilight orgy of love. For those that come from the depths of the social lie where cling the roots of human pain, joy must be an end and the end the highest aim.

I don't want to have a child that spoils my beauty and withers my youth.

I don't want to have a family that constrains my freedom. I don't want an insipid, jealous, and brutal husband who, as payment for a piece of bread, prevents the lyrical flights of the spirit through the most divine and wicked follies of lust and voluptuousness that multiple love affairs give to the flesh.

I don't love husbands and perhaps not even lovers.

I love pleasure and love.

But love is a flower that germinates on men's lips.

When I approach their lips to gather the perverse flower of love, I will do it for my love alone.

Loving the other is always needless and sometimes stupid.

It is enough to love oneself. It is enough to know how to love oneself. And I will know how to love myself so much, oh so much!

I will love myself naked in front of the mirror in the evening. I will adore myself naked in the bathtub in the morning. I will intoxicate myself naked in the arms of lovers.

Humanity walks the paths of pain in order to perpetuate itself. I walk the paths of pleasure because I seek the end.

•

I walk toward the east; I walk toward the west. I want to walk over the paths of the world gathering the flowers of love, joy and freedom.

I love black and flesh-colored stockings. White or red silk panties. Shoes of rubber and refined material. Baths in scented vinegar water, perfume from Cotty and bouquets of roses.

I want to walk over the paths of the world gathering the flowers of love, joy, and freedom.

I will break off the fronds of lime trees; I will gather hydrangea sprays, wisteria clusters, and oleander flowers to prepare the perfumed bed of my love.

And I will be the lover of vagabonds and thieves. And I will be the ideal of poets.

Because I don't want to give anything to the fatherland, to the species, and to humanity.

I want to get drunk at the fountain of pleasure, lust, and voluptuousness. I want to be completely consumed on love's pyre.

I don't want to be a mother; I don't want to be a wife. No, no, no!

Perfumed beds, lover's kisses, and the music of mad violins. Song and dance.

I know. You will call me a madwoman and a pervert. You will call me a wh...

But these are old and powerless names that no longer affect me.

I am the precocious adolescent who, after wandering in the most terrifying chasms of the depths, climbs back up to the peak to sing the sacrilegious song of my free life in the sun.

A life of beauty and strength, a life of art and love, surging with godlike sin, gushing in the sacred oasis of voluptuousness.

Enough now with epileptic frenzies of the spirit.

Nothing belongs to pagan beauty more than my young body.

Oh, love flies off with me...

Vertice, Arcola, April 21

Beyond the Two Anarchies

The social thought saturated with the revolutionary dynamic that the social-political concept of libertarian communists radiates breaks through the universal depth of human pain to intertwine in an almost monistical embrace with the higher and vaster psycho-spiritual concept of anarchist individualism yearning for the definitive and radical Anarchy.

But Anarchy being a "final absolute" in full harmony with the infinite idea and communism a "relative" social, juridical passage flowing into economic empiricism—therefore prelude and promise but not full musical harmony and epic finale—it happens that the flourishing children of the two theoretical currents of social becoming continue to wrangle, still contending with each other—now tempestuous and now calm—the philosophical-spiritual heritage of pure Anarchy. It is the ancient dualism that, dressed up again in apparent logic, still goes round in the vicious circle where the merry-go-round of dogma and utopia spin on the inauspicious axle of the dream that truth deforms and life transfigures.

And it is from this vicious circle, which neither one of the two parts has yet boldly dared to escape, that I want to decisively free myself to later immerse myself in the bath of a new sun.

The anarchist who aspires to communism and the individualist who aspires to Anarchy don't notice that they are gripped, violently, in the shackles of castrating sociology and in the jaws of the humanism that is a slimy blend of individual non-will and pseudo-christian morality.

Anyone who accepts a social, collective, and human cause is not in the pure Anarchy of the free, virgin, and original instinct of the anthropocentric inassimilables and negators.

I—anarchist and individualist—don't want to and cannot embrace the cause of atheist communism, because I don't believe in the supreme elevation of the masses and therefore I refuse the realization of Anarchy understood as a social form of human life together.

Anarchy is in free spirits, in the instinct of great rebels, and in great and superior minds.

Anarchy is the innermost animating mystery of misunderstood uniquenesses, strong because alone, noble because they have the courage of solitude and of love, aristocratic because scornful of commonness, heroic because against all...

Anarchy is nectar for the psychic I and not sociological alcohol for the collectivity.

The anarchist is the one who refuses every cause for the joy of his life radiating from inner spiritual intensity.

•

No future and no humanity, no communism and no anarchy is worthy of the sacrifice of my life. From the day that I discovered myself, I have considered myself as the supreme

PURPOSE.

Now I wrap myself in the rising trajectory of my liberated and liberating spirit, I cast off the harness of the pure nakedness of instinct to soar above the arch—ideal sociological inspiration—that joins and combines the dogmatic utopianism of the two pale dreaming anarchies to glorify— between the clash of the winds and the feasts of the sun—the egoarchic and powerful lordship of myself.

Beyond the tragic bridge of the Nietzschean overman, I catch sight of a summit even freer and more phosphorescent on which no god-man ever celebrated his birth or his easter resurrection.

Beyond the people and humanity, the absurd and sublime mystery of the undefined UNIQUE lives and throbs.

I—crazed human eagle—flash across the gloomy darkness of this black night, where the storm of ideas howls and the winds of thought roar, to later soar beyond the arms of the earliest glimmer of the dawn, among the raging flames of the noontime sun, sensing myself in the voluptuous and dionysian throbbing of the vital, amoralistic instinct where the light of the spirit and the passion of emotion get drunk in the wild and virgin springs of blood and flesh.

●

Joy is—above all—a special way of feeling life.

For the higher man who feels elevated, there is the sublime joy of sorrow and the deep sadness of happiness. Zarathustra who, through the painful and sublime solitude of the peaks, eagerly seeks the keen joy of knowledge, and encounters crazed, divine madness; Jules Bonnot who, through "Crime" and "Transgression," exalts the will of the Unique who, beyond Good and Evil, rises toward the sky of the heroic Art of living and dying; Bruno Filippi who is annihilated in the titanic effort, who claims the right of the "I" against the social constraints of the unctuous bourgeois and plebeian collectivities; these are the radiant jewels that compose the libertarian garland of my vital amoralism, as well as the protagonists of my spiritual tragedy.

In life I seek the joy of the spirit and the luxurious voluptuousness of instinct. And I don't care to know whether these have their perverse roots in the caverns of good or in the whirling abysses of evil. I rise, and if in rising I encounter the tragic lightning of my destiny, life and death will bend on my twisted lips to later follow me into the supreme turmoil where Art glorifies the strong, misunderstood rebels whom morality reviles and condemns, whom science calls lunatics, and whom society curses.

●

I am therefore the rejoicing liberated instinct. Lending an ear to myself I hear the thunderous howl of my liberator spirit that sings the epic and triumphant song of the final victory.

All ARCHIES have fallen shattered. Now I love myself, I exalt myself, I sing myself, I glorify myself. My old dreams have found rest on the pale and fragrant skin of women. My passionate, pagan mind is that of an uninhibited poet and is voluptuously reflected in their perverse eyes where the spirits of Pleasure and Evil dance the maddest dance. Only the twinkling of stars, the flowing of rivers, the whispering of forests say something of what lives in me. Anyone who can't comprehend the strange symphonies of nature can't comprehend the resounding verses of my enchanting songs.

•

Mine is not a thought or theory, but a state of mind, a particular way of feeling. When I feel the need to decisively set my Centaurs and my raging stallions free, there will be around me a mad orgy of love and blood, because I am—I feel it—what the inhabitants of the moral swamps of society call a "common criminal."

•

Madman? As you will! Normal beings have never enjoyed my affections. Among human beings, the ones I love most are the "criminals" of Thought and Action (Artists, Thieves, Vagabonds, Poets).

Among women I love the perverts. I love them dressed in blue in the evening sunset. I love them dressed in red among the golden rays of the coming dawn; I love them naked and perfumed on the bed of love, I love them dressed in white on the small bed of death.

Poor, small, great sisters of mine who I have always loved and never possessed. I love you! I love you! I love you!

Tell me, oh my living sisters, oh my deceased sisters:

who? who among you was the most famous, the greatest, the most perverted?

Ah, I remember, I remember!...

Clara, it was you!... But where are you now?

I knew you once through Octave Mirbeau's *The Torture Garden*. I knew you and I loved you! You are the strangest and most delicate creature, the most romantically and deeply human and cruel, who has known how to feel life keenly, to feel love exquisitely amidst the moaning of the tortured and the aroma of the flowers. When I think of you running, mad and light, under the blonde prelude of the golden twilight to find green sod reddened with blood and make yourself a wedding bed from it to grant yourself the deepest loving embrace, I feel exalted by admiration for you.

Ah, romantic and refined creature, how you are able to penetrate the divine miracle of flowers and how the sensual perfume of the Chinese meadow rue teaches you to exalt....

Only a great voluptuary and a great pervert could hear as your equal—still amidst the heartrending and terrible cries of the tortured—the strong and powerful voice of instinctive nature that cries: "Love yourself!... Love yourself!... Make yourself also like the flowers... In truth, there is only Love!" And I understand it and I feel it, oh Clara, your wicked and amoral love, damned and abominated by the castrated purity of the morality of the chaste and of men. I feel it, how it rises, mad and impetuous, from the most subterranean depths of instinct, to spread—with the musical harmony of eagerness and mysteries—uninhibited and superb before the cruel and barbarous spectacle of human sacrifice and to celebrate the supreme and vigorous throb of the most painfully profound JOY, resonating in the bleeding heart of the fullest, most tragic life.

●

Oh perverse heroine of Octave Mirbeau, I exalt you and sing you because I am the barbarous singer of Evil.

Above the two Anarchies of Reason and Good— glorious and triumphant—I raise the banner of the Anarchy of Instinct and Evil.

Vertice, La Spezia April 21

177

The Mysterious

written under the pseudonym of Mario Ferrento

We met on the bank of a river on a hot August afternoon. She looked at me, I looked at her...

Her fragrant, white flesh gave off the sensual perfume of all the joyful flowers and the divine light of the sun emanated from her eyes.

All human blood flowed, hot and fertile, in her azure veins, and the powerful throb of her great heart was the vast throb of all the Universe.

In her mind there was a fearful abyss containing all the darkness populated with spectral spirits of negation, and all the summits inhabited by radiant spirits of all the lights of affirmation.

She symbolized the infinite and the finite, the enigma and the truth, the revealed and the unknown, the sphinx and the mystery...

I've never seen a more perfect figure of the aimless gypsy vagabond.

She said to me: *Yes, yes, I understand that striking question mark that shines so strangely in your pupils like a diamond with malefic virtues mounted on a gold ring. Yes, yes, I understand it!...*

Do you want me to say: "We've already seen it once..."?

"In fact..." But she didn't let me finish. With a cry—she cut the word off half way and told me, *hush, hush.*

Don't speak to me of what you know, don't *speak to me of what you know, don't speak to me of what was..." And she went on: "Besides what happened to you also happened to nearly all men. You only had me in dream and very deformed!*

Vulgar story then, that of our love. But now no more dreams ... no more vulgarity!

Look at me! I am not the usual chimera, the usual creature of dreams. No! I am precisely the one who speaks to you now. Look me in the eyes!... Do you see with what hellish light my satanic pupils shine? Do you feel what perverse breath my virgin lips exude? Do you hear what strange music the rhythmic throbbings of my vast heart compose? And the mad, tremendous mystery of this frightful mind of mine, do you understand it?

•

I was disoriented. I believed that some excess of delirium or some wave of joy had given me hallucinations.

I take my eyes from hers and look at the river's waters that flow majestically in the furrow of their bed silent as the purest silver liquid.

Among the green herbal shrubs populating the bank, little creeping shadows played tag—amid the dancing of the wind—with the slender slivers of sun.

The domestic field and the wild forest interweave—at a small distance—the majestic and joyful choruses of their superb songs.

She—the Mysterious One—continued to talk to me this way: *I have seen you pale and sad, but with eyes that foresaw radiant with hope, descending into the deepest labyrinths of human sorrow to gather some precious gems, scattered among the debris of ancient mines dug in way back in time by ancient miners.*

But every stone gathered made your hands bleed and every cavern penetrated showed you the monstrous face of Doubt between whose jaws your mind was gripped as in an atrocious bite.

You thought:—And what if the gathered stone was fake? and what if my efforts were in vain?—But when you then discovered the radiant brilliance of another gem, hidden among the useless debris, then immediately the joy of the labor flooded you again with its thousands of varied frenzies, and you dug feverishly, heedless of the sweat that bathed your forehead and of the blood that gushed through your heart. And when you had placed all the precious stones of ancient knowledge on the altar of the pagan mind, you opened wide the wings of the new thought to fly up to the peak of the ideal to quench your thirst at the pure spring of faith.

179

But when you sat on the absolute peak, satisfied with your great conquests, here it was that the furies of doubt called together that black demon of melancholy to scale the mountain and attack you in your sacred hermitage.

Then you noticed that you had not found the luminous way of true peace and your pupils, black and lost, gazed intensely into the void.

Ah, yes! You sought the WAY, poor madman. But the way does not exist....

There are many ways, but not the one way! And you were the on way. You with your great defects and your great virtues.

But you didn't see yourself... You were a discoverer of unknown worlds but you didn't discover yourself. You who was the animating center of all worlds.

You were never the great monological loner, forgotten by the world, and God and contemplater of yourself.

I have seen materialists crawl through the bowels of the earth like black reptiles, and the spiritualists (idealists) fly, transported and empty like miserable, dried out perfections. And behind them I have seen the long contingent of mystics and the infinite theories of ascetics, wandering—poor lunatics—in search of external laws to serve in a damp and moldy sewer of theory overshadowed by faith, in which to channel their useless life as possessed people!

The human being—even the one who carried the flag of Freedom in his fist—always seeks for slavery in life.

No one wants to be convinced of a reality that negates every 'system,' every 'rule,' every 'form.'

Even libertarians seek the system, the rule, the form.

They seek the emasculating theory and the murderous faith. Try telling them: neither 'rules' nor 'forms' nor 'systems,' but Thrills and Quivers, Sensitivity and Intuition, Lyricism and Imagination, Force and Fantasy, and they will tell you: 'Society requires something else completely, Humanity requires something else completely!

Society and Humanity are the nightmare of the possessed. And this tormenting nightmare of Society and of 'requires...' creates the dark armies of the pessimists that see everything as black and those of the optimists who see everything as rosy.

The world is—for itself—the same thing as all. But skeptics don't believe and the religious worship. But both are rabidly stubborn and condemn the one who knows how to be religious and atheist, saint and sinner, skeptic and believer, rebel and dominator all at the same time. And this is simply because no one wants to understand that the being is an all in all and not an infinitesimal particle of the universe or a microscopic cog in the human machine. And you also—my poor madman—seek a way, a horizon, an 'over there' to your life. But all ways are open to the vagabond of the spirit, as every temple is vulnerable for the iconoclast and every destiny possible to the Hero.

There isn't a WAY but there are all WAYS.

There isn't a Truth but there are all Truths.

There isn't right but Force.

There isn't law but free will.

There isn't Justice but Injustice

There isn't the thing that's called Love but rather Egoism.

All theoretical coherence is mutilation of life and true logic is illogicality. Every human being who follows a way with his eyes fixed on a goal is always in the company of remorse like the one who on swearing an oath always finds regret.

Only the one who walks on all paths with his eye fixed on the disc of his inner world can be the lord of serenity and the God of happy peace.

Here the Mysterious One paused. She looked around. She looked at the beautiful sun, the crystalline river and the festive forest. She sang an atheist hymn to the solitude that has no witnesses. Then she playfully told me: *Yes, I am yours, all yours. This is the place in which you should take me.* And having said this she transformed into the form of a shadow and, approaching me, penetrated me. From that day, I am her body since She is nothing else but my Mind.

Vertice, La Spezia April 21

1922

Black Flags

Black flags in the wind
stained with blood and sun
Black flags in the sun
howling of glory in the wind
We need to return to the sources. To drink at the ancient fountains.
We need to return to heroic anarchism, to individual, violent, reckless, poetic, decentering audacity...
And we need to return with every bit of our modern instinct, every bit of our new conception of life and beauty, every bit of our healthy and lucid pessimism, which is not renunciation or powerlessness, but a thriving flower of exuberant life. We are the true nihilists of reality and the spiritual builders of ideal worlds.
We are destructive philosophers and creative poets.
We walk in the night
with a sun in our mind
and with two huge golden stars
in our blazing eyes
We walk...

2

Several years ago, all the earth's kings, all the world's tyrants crossed the threshold of time, and—turning their backs on the dawn—called in a great voice—the ghosts of the past, of the gloomiest past!
The voices of the tyrants and kings were joined by the raucous voices of all the great misers of the spirit, of art, of thought and of the idea!—And in the voices of the tyrants, kings and misers, ghosts and phantoms were raised from their tombs

and came to dance among us...

The "state," the "race," the "fatherland" were macabre storm clouds assailing the heavens, ghastly phantoms darkening the sun; they threw us back into the dark night of distant medieval times.

3

Death!

Who still recalls the macabre dance of the baleful and monstrous god of war?

Who still recalls the war?

Much time has passed between then and now, but upon this wretched yet noble earth, fertilized with sterile corpses and bloated with infertile blood, not a single, ideal, virgin flower, made of spirituality and purity, still sprouts today.

No, the flowers that are born now on the dry clods of this earth, so vainly bathed in blood, are not flowers of flourishing life, capable of great hope, virile struggle, vigorous thought; they are rather flowers of death, born in the shadow, growing in the anguish of the unconscious, swept away in the hurricane, borne along in the drift of the river of oblivion...

...

I am not a sentimentalist... but I have a horrible memory of the war.

It is the reason that I ended up hating and then despising men. Before despising and hating them though, I collected all the tears of humanity in my heart and locked all the sorrows of the world in my vast mind-synthesis...

...

Even the spirit of the great Zarathustra—who is war's truest lover and the warrior's most sincere friend—must have been horribly nauseated by this war...

He must have been horribly nauseated, because I heard him cry

186

out: "You must seek your own enemy, fight your own war, and for your own ideas!"

And if your idea succumbs, may your rectitude cry out in triumph.

But, alas! the heroic preaching of the great liberator came to nothing!

The human herd didn't know how to distinguish its own enemy or to fight its own war for its own ideas. (The herd has no ideas of its own!)

And not knowing his own ideas that he might make triumph, Abel died at Cain's hands once again.

He was called to die, and he went, like always. So!

Without knowing how to say either Yes or No! He goes as a coward, as a robot, like always.

If he had at least had the capacity to say the Yes of enthusiastic obedience—if he didn't have the heroic power to pronounce the titanic No of tragic negation—he would at last have shown that he believed in the "cause" for which he died, fighting... but he didn't know how to say yes or no!

He went!

As a coward, like always!

So...

And when he left, he went toward death.

He went toward death without knowing why. Like always!

And death did not wait...

It came!... It came and danced.

It danced and laughed!

For five long years...

It laughed and danced over the muddy trenches of the entire world's fatherlands.

A macabre dance!

Oh, how idiotic and vulgar—how savage and brutal—is this death that dances without the wings of an idea on its back.

Without a violent idea that smashes and destroys.

Without a fruitful idea that generates and creates.

What a stupid and horrendous thing, dying as cowards, without knowing why.

We saw it—as it danced—Death.

It was a black Death, opaque, without any of the transparency of light.

It was a Death without wings!... How ugly and vulgar it was.

How clumsy its dance was!

And how it mowed them down—dancing—all the superfluous, those of whom there were more!

Those for whom—the great liberator says—the state was invented.

But, alas, it didn't only mow these down...

Yes! Death, to avenge the state, mowed down those who were not useless, those who were necessary...

It also mowed down those for whom life was a profound poem where sublimated sorrow sang a playful refrain... But those of whom there were not more, those who were not superfluous, those who fell crying out the rebellious and forceful titanic No!: they will be avenged.

We will avenge them!

We will avenge them because they were our brothers; because they died with stars in their eyes; because as they died, they drank the sun.

The sun of the Dream.

The sun of Battle.

The sun of Life.

The sun of the Idea!

4

The war!...

What has the war renewed?

Where is the heroic transfiguration of the spirit?

Where have the phosphorescent tablets of new human values been hung?

In what sacred temple have the miraculous gold amphorae, containing the flaming hearts of creative geniuses and dominating heroes, promised by the frantic supporters of great war?

Where does the majestic sun of the great new dawn shine? Frightful rivers of blood washed all the turf in the world and went howling through all the paths of the earth.

Terrifying torrents of tears made their heartrending, anguished lament echo through the darkest, most remote eddies of all the world's continents.

Mountains of human bones and flesh rotted everywhere in the mud, and cried everywhere in the sun.

But nothing changed—it was useless!

The worm-ridden bourgeois belly just belched with satiety! and that of the proletarian howled from too much hunger!

And enough!

If with Christ and christianity, the human spirit was suspended in the cold and empty void of the afterlife, with Karl Marx and socialism it was made to descend into the intestines... The roar that sounded across the world after the war, shaking humanity, was nothing but a belly roar that socialism betrayed, stamped out, smothered, strangled, as soon as it noticed that this roar had begun to take on a bit of the color of an ideal content...

This supreme, nameless cowardice used up, the blackest, bleakest, most baleful reaction was born and grew tremendously.

It was logical—natural—fatal! It was human...

5

Our time—despite empty and contrary appearances—is already lying on all fours under the heavy wheels of a new History.

The bestial morality of our bastard christian-liberal-bourgeois-plebeian civilization turns toward the sunset... Our false social organization is collapsing fatally—inexorably! The fascist phenomenon is the surest, most indisputable proof of it.

In Italy as elsewhere…

To show it, one would only have to go back in time and question history. But even this isn't necessary!—The present speaks eloquently enough…

Fascism is nothing but a cruel, convulsive spasm of a decaying society that tragically drowns in the quagmire of its lies. Because it—fascism—indeed celebrates its bacchanals with flaming pyres and malicious orgies of blood; but the dull crackling of its livid fires doesn't give off a single spark of vivid innovative spirituality; meanwhile, may the blood that pours out be transformed into wine, that we—the forerunners of the time—silently gather in red goblets of hatred setting it aside as the heroic beverage to pass on to the children of the night and of sorrow in the fatal communion of great revolt.

We will take these brothers of ours by the hand to march together and climb together toward new spiritual dawns, toward new auroras of life, toward new conquests of thought, toward new feasts of light; new solar noons.

Because we are lovers of liberating struggle.

We are the children of sorrow that rises and thought that creates.

We are restless vagabonds.

The boldest in every endeavor; the tempter of every ordeal.

And life is an "ordeal"! A torment! A tragic flight.—A fleeting moment!

6

Our will is heroic!

We'll stir everything up in a flurry of hatred at the heart of the world, and we'll transmute everything into a storm of the abyss.

Into a hurricane of the peaks.

Into cries of the mind.

Into howls of freedom!

By celebrating the social evensong, we will try to fully realize individual life, of the free and great I.

So that the night no longer triumphs.

So that the shadow no longer coils around us.

So that the never-ending fire of the sun becomes eternal and perpetuates its feast of light over land and sea!

Because we are fiery dreamers of the impossible, dangerous conquerors of the stars!

7

Fascism—despite empty and contrary appearances—is something far too ephemeral and impotent to prevent the free, unbridled course of rebel thought that overflows and expands, impetuously bursting beyond every barrier, and furiously spreads beyond every limit—as a powerful, animating, driving force—drawing behind its gigantic steps the

vigorous and titanic action of hard human muscle.

Fascism is impotent, because it is brute force.

It is matter without spirit.

It is body without mind.

It is night without dawn!

It—fascism—is the other face of socialism... They are lightless mirrors. Two spent stars!

Socialism is the numerical—material—force that, by acting in the shadow of a dogma, resolves and dissolves itself in a miserable spiritual "no" that empties it of any unchained, willful, heroic, ideal resilience. Fascism is an epileptic child of the spiritual "no" that is brutalized by striving—vainly— toward a vulgar material "yes."

In the field of moral values, they are equal. Fascism and socialism are two worthy brothers. Even if you call the latter Abel and you call the former Cain. A common Dream unites them.

And that dream is called Power.

8

Black flags in the wind
stained with blood and sun
Black flags in the sun
howling of glory in the wind

What the war didn't and couldn't do, revolution can and must do!

Oh, black flags carried
in a man's rebellious fist
as he focuses his gaze intensely
beyond the ruling lie
—fluttering in the sun and wind
fluttering in the wind and sun
Victory smiles in the distance!
In the distance—in the distance—in the distance!
In the glory of the sun and wind!

9

Fascism and socialism are bandages of the time, delayers of the deed!
They are rabidly crystallized fossils that willful dynamism— with
   which we animate history as it passes—will sweep away into
   the common grave of the times.—Because in the field of spiritual and ethical values the two enemies are the same.
They are two sides of the same coin.
They both lack the light of eternity!
Only great intellectual vagabonds—carriers of the black flag—can
   be the luminous animating fulcrum of eternal revolution that
   pushes the world forward.

10

Our willful soul is multiform...
The fiery throbbing of the sun and the tremulous shudders of the
    stars pass through it!
We are rebel poets and philosophers of destruction.
We are anarchists. Iconoclasts! Individualists, atheists, nihilists!
We are the carriers of black flags.

We walk in the night
with a sun in our mind,
and with two huge golden stars
shining in our blazing eyes!
We walk on!...

And in the theater of humanity, our place is at the most extreme of
    all extreme lefts.

11

Behind the gigantic, black thundercloud that still covers the sky, a
    red twilight flashes.
The tragic celebration of the red evensong is near.
The last black night will become red with blood.
With blood and fire.
Because blood demands blood. It's an old story...
And then our children—the children of the Dawn—must be born
    from blood and forged by fire.
Because new individual ideas must be born, more virginal and
    beautiful, from the great social tragedies, from the turmoil of
    new hurricanes!
And it is only from the great, fiery, bloody catastrophe that the real,
    profound Antichrist of humanity and thought will be born.
    The real child of earth and sun able to climb over the peaks

and probe the abysses.

Because the Antichrist is Eagle and Serpent.

He inhabits the peaks and the depths.

He—the spirit of the new man—will pass through the smoking ruins of the old, destroyed world to rise toward the magnificent mystery of the coming virgin dawn.

Beautiful and superb—he will stand upon the threshold of the new morning saturated with the wild, scintillating strength of superhuman beauty, saying to reluctant men:

Onward, onward!

We rush beyond every system
We rush beyond every form
We fly toward the highest freedom
Toward extreme ANARCHY!

12

We—free spirits—vagabonds of the idea—atheists of solitude—demons of the unseen desert.

We—luminous monsters of the night—we have already gone to the peaks.

We walk in the night
with a sun in our mind,
and with two huge golden stars
shining in our blazing eyes!

And—with us—everything must be driven to its highest consequence.

Even hatred.

Even violence.

Even "crime"!

Because hatred gives strength that dares.

Violence and "crime" are the genius that destroys and the beauty that creates.

And we want to dare.

To destroy—to renew—to create!

Because all that is low and vulgar must be broken up and destroyed.

Only what is great shall remain.

Because what is great belongs to beauty.

And life should be beautiful.

Even in sorrow.

Even in the hurricane!...

13

We have killed the "duty" of solidarity, so that our free lust for spontaneous love and voluntary parenthood acquires a heroic value in life.

We killed pity because it is a false christian emotion and because we want to create noble, unacknowledged generous egoism.

We strangled false social rights—creator of the humble, cowardly beggars—so that man will dig up his deepest, most secret "I" to find the power of the Unique.

Because we know it ourselves.

Life is tired of having stunted lovers.

Because the earth is tired of being uselessly trampled by huge hordes of stupid, chanting, praying, christian midgets.

And finally because we are also tired of these carrion "brothers" of ours who are incapable of peace or war. Inferior in hatred and in love.

Yes! We are sick and tired!

Humanity must be renewed.

We need an epic and barbaric song of new and virgin life sounding over the world.

We're the carriers
of blazing torches.
We're the kindlers of crackling pyres.
Our flag is black.
Our road is the infinite.
And our highest ideal
is the peak and the abyss.

We walk on!...

We walk in the night
with a sun in our mind,
and with two huge golden stars
shining in our blazing eyes!

We walk on...
And if our dream is an illusion?
And if our struggles are useless and vain? And if the renewal of
    humanity is impossible to accomplish?
Ah, no! We will walk on just the same.
For our own dignity.
For the love of our ideas.
For the freedom of our spirits.
For the passion of our minds.
For the necessity of our life.
Better to die as heroes in an effort of liberation and selfelevation
    than to vegetate as impotent cowards in this repugnant reality.

Oh black flags,
oh black trophies,
emblems and symbols
of eternal revolt.

You who are the bloody evidence of all human audacity:
You who are the destroyers of all prejudice:
You who are the only real enemies of all human shame—of all sin-
    ister lies!
You who sing eternal revolt, soaked in sorrow and blood!

I grip it in my strong fist
and in the midst of windy storms
I raise it in the glory of the sun.
In the glory of sun and the wind...
Of wind and sun and light.

Il Proletario, vol.1, no.2, Potremoli, July

Of Individualism and Rebellion

There are those who maintain that the human being is by nature a social being. Others maintain that the human being is by nature anti-social.

Well, I admit that I have never been able to clearly understand what they meant by their "by nature," but I have understood that both sides are wrong, since the human being is social and anti-social at the same time.

Need, want, affection, love, and sympathy are the elements that push him toward sociability and union.

The craving for independence and the desire for freedom push her toward solitude and individualism. But, while individualism operates and is realized against society, society defends itself from its attacks. The war between "societarianism" and "individualism" is thus a fertile war of vitality and energy. But, while the individual is necessary to society, this in its turn is necessary to him.

Individualism couldn't possibly exist if there were no society against which it could affirm itself and live, expand itself and rejoice.

•

Among human beings—only the rebel is the most beautiful figure and the most complete being. He knows how to be the potential tool of his desiring will. He knows how to obey himself and command himself, to preserve himself and destroy himself. Because the rebel is the one who has learned the secret of living and the art of dying.

•

The one who falls rebelling against each and all, prevails even while falling.

And prevailing means instilling the flame of her thought and imposing the light of her ideas in others.

But the fallen rebel's truest follower is the one who, when

falling, knows how to rebel even against the "rebellion" of the already fallen hero.

•

Anyone who wants the spirit of rebellion to become eternal must want the child's rebellion not to change in its turn into the father's tyranny.

•

If my father rebelled against my grandfather so as not to be a slave of the paternal faith, I rebel against my father so as not to be a slave of the faith that made him rebel in his turn.

How could it make my son be tomorrow what I am today?

•

Only from the ruins of everything the rebel has destroyed can the creative genius be born.

But what does the creation of the genius prepare if not a new rebellion?

•

I agree with Nietzsche in believing that there has never been any need to question a martyr to know the truth. But desiring force, daring audacity and skillful creative will are treasures inherited only from the genius, the rebel, the hero.

•

I have seen a genius "steal" and an idiot throw a deadly bomb at a state minister.

The first stole so as to live independently and create in freedom. The second killed because of a hidden personal hatred and the will to die.

The first carried out a "vulgar, common crime" and is a "common criminal." The second carried out a "political crime" and is a "noble and generous political criminal." I now ask all subversive, political people in general, and anarchists in particular—if in facing this fact, it is a chance to raise another "political crime" up into the splendor of glory and the feasts of the sun so as to cast "common crime" into the mud.

•

Alas! There are still too many who look at the work. But before looking at the work, I look at the creator. Yet even for many—so many—anarchists, it seems that the individual counts for little...

The majority of them are still among the rabble who say: "Human beings don't count. Events and ideas count." And this is why, even among us, many higher, sublime beings have been cast into the mud, while many idiots have been raised up in the sun.

•

I deny the right to judge me to all those who don't understand the voice of my yearnings, the howl of my needs, the flights of my spirit, the sorrow of my mind, the thrill of my ideas, and the anguish of my thought. But only I understand all this. Do you want to judge me? Okay then! But you will never judge my real self. Instead you will judge the "me" that you yourself have invented. When you believe you have me between your fingers to crush me, I will be up there, laughing in the distance.

Il Proletario, vol.1, no.4, Pontremoli, September 17

A "Female"

I love you most of all, when the joy flees from
your oppressed brow; when your heart drowns
itself in horror, when the horrible cloud
of the past extends over your present.
—Charles Baudelaire

I am a strange, cursed poet.

Everything that is abnormal and perverse has a morbid allure for me.

My spirit—a venomous butterfly with divine features—is attracted to the sinful scents that waft out from the flowers of evil.

Today I sing of the perverse beauty of a "female"— of one of our females that I have never possessed and will never possess...

Now she wanders, nameless, forgotten, and ignored, through the twisted paths of life, with such a deep, dark sorrow locked inside her heart that it raises her above Women and makes her divine.

This great flower of evil—contaminated and contaminating—holds so much human purity within itself that it sublimates a life, making it divine.

●

Female?

Yes; perhaps!

●

A strange tale circulates around her name. It says: Her beautiful and wicked body languished in the arms of vagabonds and thieves, late night revelers and poets, rebels and heroes...

All the monsters of the night knew the voluptuous secrets of her pale flesh...

All those thirsty for love drank from her lips...

But wherever she passed, she left broken hearts and bleeding minds, weeping flesh and spirits in revolt...

For she—this madwoman—was—like Zarathustra's poem—a

dionysian Harp of voluptuousness for everyone and for no one.

While her wicked and trembling body lay wrapped in voluptuous spasms on the bed of love, swept away in the great chasms of devotion, her restless, vagabond, rebel spirit wandered through the endless regions of the infinite to give body to an intangible, ethereal dream. Her mind, sick from solitude and distance, never let itself be swept away by the spasmodic fever of her insatiable flesh...

She loved only herself...

•

One of those who held the fragrant, perverse body of this pale "Female" in his arms cast into her—unfortunately fertile—womb the fatal seeds of another most unhappy life. Under the imperious commandment of Nature, the "Female" became Mother. And society, which had been unjust, vindictive, and cruel to the Female, was also against the Mother and even the child. Alone and powerless—he was thrown into the overwhelming storm of life, prey to the saddest loneliness that comes from misery and desperation.

The mother, alone, mocked, persecuted, cursed, scorned. He, sad and melancholy, was a premature victim in his turn.

•

I focus my eyes on the mysterious dawn of this strange Female mind, so that I can gather its dispersed ruin and reconstruct its secret.

I know that beneath the dionysian playfulness of these perverse and dissolute creatures, a fine thread of mysterious melancholy almost always runs...

Through my reconstructive poetic imagination, I again see the adolescent virgin when the hot, perverse sun of voluptuousness and pleasure first plunged like a golden blade into her flesh that throbbed with desire, making the irresistible cry of exuberant youth thunder in her mind: love, love, love!

It may have been a mild, fair dawn; it may have been a red twilight.

She gave herself to the first loving embrace, and from that day, her body was a Harp of voluptuousness, a poem of pleasure, seized by pagan fire; a hymn of intoxication sung beyond good and evil, where free spirits celebrate the iconoclastic rite to the joy of human life.

But beneath the dionysian playfulness of this perverse and dissolute creature ran a fine thread of mysterious melancholy.

One day—perhaps one of those sad days when the stars, by means of their occult, magnetic forces, forewarn a being of the dark fatality of his destiny—on a path swarming with people in a large, noisy city, three or four pistol shots rang out.

A pale youth reached the horrendous peak of the most tragic desperation, before falling, exhausted and defeated, into the mud on the path. He wanted to make an unfeeling humanity that ignores everything hear the dark thunder of his protest.

A sad and tragic thing.

Together with a member of shameful humanity, a comrade in vengeance falls.

Who was the pale youth who transformed his slender, lily-white hand into an avenger's claw?

The son of the rebel Female, of the uninhibited one!

•

At the tragic announcement, the perverse Female bent over like a melancholy weeping willow under the raging hurricane, and was purified in the great sorrow of the Mother who was mortally wounded in the most intimate and secret of all her emotions! The voluptuous flower of evil cleanses its soul, perhaps impure but beautiful, in the divine and blessed dew of weeping, and becomes a lilac-flower of pure and uncontaminated beauty.

That unfeeling mind of hers, which no one had ever fully possessed, was reserved to gather the great sorrow that the son of her own belly had to bring her in order to avenge her while avenging himself.

•

The dissolute and playful "Female" is now the lonely, nameless Mother, locked in the circle of her sorrow, silent and tragic like an impenetrable sphinx who walks the polluted paths of life, maybe pardoning, maybe cursing...

The raging Anarchy of her free instinct has merged with the delicate sensibility of her new maternal emotion, and from the condensation of these two deeply human elements a spirituality must now shine that is so enchanting that it radiates utterly unknown constellations of human sorrow.

I open my mouth wide toward the unknown and loudly call to this Female-mother, greeting her with the name of Sister!

"Woman"?

What does she matter to me?

This Female now lives beyond her: on a higher peak!

I love the dissolute and playful creatures beneath whose dionysian paganism a fine thread of mysterious melancholy runs; and I love them best when the horrible cloud of their past extends itself over their present...

Il Proletario, vol.1, no.1, Pontremoli, June 5

With Sincere Pity

To "the Goliard"[18] of *Umanità Nova*[19]

> *I strike you without anger or hatred, like a*
> *butcher, like Moses struck the rock!*
> —Charles Baudelaire

Oh, good "Goliard", come—come to me!

Come and listen to the sublime verses of my perverse, cursed lyre. Come and listen to the laughter of my melancholy...

What are you afraid of? What are you afraid of?

Could you be afraid of the livid, yellow fires of my sulfurous hells?

Could you be afraid of the mysterious winds of my symbolic peaks?

Don't you understand me?

"Couldn't I be a false chord in the divine symphony, thanks to the consuming irony that shakes and bites me?" But you, who are you?

Could you be some spectacled professor who still has old polemical-theoretical accounts to settle with me?

But let it go, oh Goliard, let go of ancient regrets and old torments that trouble your heart. Today is my spiritual Easter feast, my table is set...

So come—oh Goliard—to my table, drink and be quiet!

2

I am a "well of truth, black and shining, where the livid star, the

---

18   A Goliard was a wandering clerical student in medieval Europe disposed to conviviality, license, and the making of ribald and satirical Latin songs.
19   The paper of the Italian Anarchist Federation. I believe it is still being published and has generally followed a Malatestan line.

ironic, hellish beacon, the torch of satanic charm, sole glory and comfort—the awareness in evil—flickers!" But you—who are you?

"Lucky for them, the workers don't know Baudelaire." What did you say? Is that how it is, true Goliard? "Long live ignorance and Anarchy. Death to intellectuality, Thought, and Art." Is this what you mean, true Goliard?

But doesn't "Goliard" signify the rebellious and dissolute student of the Middle Ages?

Ah, poor, grotesque parody! Oh! pity... pity!

3

Certain that the good *Umanitá Nova* will absolve and that the Sacred Vestal Virgin—of whom you are the zealous priest—will pardon you, I—the "perverse" and "cursed" poet—invite you into my sad, melancholy oasis where unknown springs gush coolly.

Oh! Come, come!

My demon sleeps too much today and so do my pure Furies.[20]

Come, come...

I will show you the purest flowers of evil in the human garden of my heart, under the fruitful sun of my tormented soul. They are flowers of pity and sorrow, they are roses of blood and love, they are shudders and tears.

Tears of flesh and shudders of the ideal—music of urgent life, flights of spirituality...

Oh, come, come...

Today, in my hell, there is Paradise—come, oh Goliard, it is time!

---

20   A reference to the *Erinyes* or Furies of ancient Greek mythology, dark, primal goddesses of vengeance.

4

Here is the "damned Woman" whose sorrowful beauty I artistically—anarchically, humanely, sensitively—sang, whose tortured mind I raised—in song. Look at her, look at her. Do you see her, oh Goliard?

Do you hear her?

Look! There are the ones "laid on the sand, like a thoughtful herd, who turn their eyes toward the mountainous horizon," and others are "deep in the woods stammering the loves of timid childhood." Do you see them?

Watch, oh Goliard, as they "walk through rocks full of phantasms!" That is where Saint Anthony saw the blushing naked breasts of his temptation rise like lava...

And then there are those with "howling fevers" who call on Bacchus to drown their regrets, and others who "hide a horsewhip under their dresses" to then—in the dark forest and on solitary nights—"mix the froth of pleasure with their tears and torments." And I—oh, Goliard of *Umanitá Nova,* who tried to make unconscious mockery and irony about what I wrote that you couldn't understand—I wanted to sing of one of these "damned women"— all women are, in this sense, more or less "damned"—one of those who, like the poet, is able to say, "Skies, lacerated like seahores, my pride is reflected in you.

"Your vast clouds, in mourning, are the funeral cars of my dreams, and your glimmerings are the reflections of the Hell in which my heart revels."

5

Charles Baudelaire, the man who—"lucky for them"— "the workers don't know." The marvelous poet who, without the treasury of the U.A.I. in his pocket, was able to get intoxicated with the most exquisite—even though dangerous—deep, luminous, refined sensations. The singular genius whose "mysteriously half-opened lips seemed to guard sarcastic secrets." The strange, cursed, god-like poet who had no horror of bending down in the mud to humanely gather the Flowers of Evil and sublimate them through the tragic glow of his Art, so that he sang those "damned women" over the tremulous bow of his magical lyre.

"Oh virgins, oh demons, oh monsters, oh martyrs, great spirits, contemptuous of reality, thirsty the infinite, devotees and bacchantes, now full of howls and tears, you, who my spirit has followed into your hell, poor sisters, I love you as I sympathize with you, with your dark pain, with your unsatisfied thirst and the urns of love that fill your great hearts!"

6

And I too—like Baudelaire, one of the great dead ones whom I secretly love—I desired—in the columns of this paper of ours—that is guilty of being called *Proletario*—to sing—humanely and anarchically—the tragedy, the tears, the laughter, the crying, the sorrow, the torment, the good, the evil, the sin, and the hope of one of these women so that anarchists will know that, among us, not everyone is willing to throw mud and shit on those who, through an excessive thirst for the infinite, have fallen headlong into the abyss with their eyes fixed on the sky and their minds intoxicated by the stars.

And I have written this all with a pen that is my own, with a language that is my own, with a style that is original, that is my own, and that no goliardic—poorly goliardic— irony could persuade me to change by turning from my path.

7

Some comrade—writing privately to another comrade—once characterized Renzo Novatore as "Anarchy's Guido da Verona."[21] Without pausing to refute the accusation, I will say to you, as Guido da Verona had to say to his critics: "Say what you will about me, I will always give you fragrant roses... even if born in sorrow, even if germinated in tears."

8

Today, my anarchist heart is full of infinite kindness. My winged mind wanders round and round through the sky of the idea.

My free spirit dances merrily in the sad oasis of my solitude—where my mysterious melancholy sings.

Come, oh Goliard—come!

Today my demon is sleeping, as are my Furies...

Come drink at the unknown, virgin springs of my infinite pity...

Tomorrow, the satanic creatures of my volcanic hell could awaken, and I could be furious...

You know? I am a strange, many-sided man.

Proletario, no.3, August 15

---

21   Guido da Verona (1881-1939) was a poet and erotic novelist who eventually got into trouble with the fascist authorities for his writings and committed suicide to escape death at their hands.

Noontime Songs

Verily, there is yet a future for evil too.
And the hottest noon has not yet been discovered for man.
—F. Nietzsche, *Thus Spoke Zarathustra*[22]

I am alone, I am alone! Alone and distant... But what does it all matter?

Yes, what does it matter to me?

The vast and boundless wilderness stretches out around me, and here—amid the sun's golden rays—firs and pines sing their strange songs composed from symphonies of silence and the music of mystery... I am singing too.

I am singing the song of my bleeding truths for all the blood-stained minds. I am singing the song of my greatest, most desperate noon: I am singing the dog day poem of my hottest summer!...

But I sing only for my solitary and unknown comrades; I sing only for my distant children...

For my heart is no longer a spring garden dotted with fragile and fragrant roses; for my heart is no longer a vermilion jewel box full of virgin dreams.

Anyone who has sung the morning poem must sing the noontime poem. And I am singing it! I am singing the dog day songs of my hot summer.

2

Once I dreamed...

It was the first joyful spring of my youth! Those were good

---

22   I have chosen to translate this as it appears in the Italian, where "noon" is used in place of "south," because obviously Novatore is playing on the word "noon."

times!...

A mysterious ideal flapped its invisible wings over the ethereal waves; fleshy tears were enlightened by spiritual laughter; within me, human sorrow was transformed into a harmonic dream of future beauty!...

I dreamed great dreams of justice and freedom... of brotherhood and love...

And I lived for this dream; I fought for this dream...

My mind was completely covered with fragile, fragrant roses, and my heart was a vermilion jewel box full of virgin dreams!...

My eyes glowed with a red and golden light, and my faith was a dramatic, emotional "Yes" that believed and hoped...

Yes! Then I believed...

I believed in brotherhood; in human redemption; in love...

"The self-elevation of men..." "Elevation of the masses..." "Ascent of the people..." "Sublimation of humanity!..." Ah! that great poem of dreams, my youth!

3

Along the path of all those born to great and generous labors—to the promethean "virtues" of thought—there is a liberating demon hiding, waiting in ambush.

I also had my hidden demon, and one day he was ly-ing in wait for me, smiling and sure...

He told me, *I am the eagle in the heights and the diver in the depths...*

I come from past eternity and head toward future eternity.

I am eternal Evil, because I am Sorrow. I am the tragic No! that perpetuates itself. The negating and demolishing spirit; the liberating and creating revolt!...

I am man's roots, the I of life. I am the negating spirit of your most subterranean depths. And when I come out from my frightful cavern to ride the centaurs of the wind and make my truths howl over the world's back, phantoms die and men grow pale.

4

The demon told me this about my most subterranean depths. This one who is able to tell terrible truths that draw blood...

Once god was the tyrant.

Then came the family and society, the people and humanity!

But I spoke with one who comes from past eternity and is heading toward future eternity...

And I recognize these baleful phantoms...

Ah, and I have seen them drink so many rivers of blood, sweat, and tears along the road of the centuries!...

I have seen them devour so many mountains of corpses!...

So many!...

And every dead person who fell whispered "Tomorrow!"

"Tomorrow?" "God and tomorrow" "Humanity and tomorrow" "The people and tomorrow." But today?

So where is my hero?

—Where are my solitary and unknown brothers, where are my distant children, those—either geniuses or maniacs— who know how to live and die alone and liberated, shouting—consciously and knowingly: "I" "Today" "My freedom" "My realization"?

5

I am alone, I am alone! Alone and distant...

A high fever hammers my brow, and a new thirst burns me; it burns my mouth...

The plebeian wells are now too far for me, and the virgin springs are still unknown mysteries to me... I am still an Arc.

When will I be a Peak?

...

The light of dusk.

I hear a bird's song; I watch it fly through the melan-choly clearness of an agonic Evensong and dissipate below in the velvet blue of distant shadows.

From a certain association of ideas, I also seem to see the winged dreams of my youth dissipating down there in the distance, far away among the sad, mournful shadows of oblivion...

6

It was nothing. A nostalgic shadow of memory merely passed through the vivid light of the dog-day morning of my hot summer day.

Now it's all passed. The fever hammered my brow, the thirst burnt my mouth. I bent myself over the cause of my "need" and my "thirst," quenching them in the springs of my hot blood and the rain of my bitter sweat. This pungent selfdrinking made me intoxicated with a mad delirium that exalts and transforms.

Now the miracle of my noontime tragedy is accomplished.

I have fallen like an Arc, I rise up like a peak into the mystery of the wind and the glory of the sun to speak the heroic words of my exalted transformation and my madness.

7

I spoke with the shade of my "first" solitude. She told me: *You dreamed brotherhood with your eyes closed in the fog of faith, but when you opened them in the sun of reality, you saw the tragic drama of Cain and Abel.*

I spoke with the shade of my "second" solitude, and she told me: *You called for pure friendship so sincerely, but when*

you eagerly strained your ears to hear the answer to your call, you heard a sharp, metallic jingle answer you. It was the vile sound of Judas' thirty silver coins, still sounding over the world.

I spoke with the shade of my "third" solitude, and she told me: *You desperately called for real solidarity between all human beings, and at your desperate cry, sardonic, sinister laughter, made of slander and scorn, answered.*

I spoke with the shade of my "fourth" solitude, and she told me: *You addressed so many songs and poems to the love between man and woman, but this love has become a covert war between the sexes.*

I spoke with the shade of my "fifth" solitude, and she told me: *You believed that the I could become the we, because man needs society.*

But don't you see that this need is precisely what makes man a slave and unhappy? Did you think there was a way? But there was no way... Life is a closed circle (paved with the dead weight of the many and blocked by the eternally brutish majority) within which man is damned to a perpetual war of vital conquest and individual possession. The living man has never had, does not have, and will not have anything but what his individual force and his own capacity for power authorize him to have. And since—like you my malicious reader—I dropped my head at this statement, my fifth solitude began to talk again, continuing like this:—*Woe to anyone who, from pity or compassion for his old self, fears the light of the new I that is coming. You tremble with dismay and fright. You are unsure and indecisive like something trembling on the edge of an abyss... Could you be a christian nihilist? Does the tragic fatality that weighs on the reality of life frighten you? Could you be one of my enemies? Well, if so, lay your cause—like good christians—beyond life; but I teach placing life beyond good and evil. There, where the liberated I throbs and blazes. There, where the negating spirit rises up against the idea of society and condemns it; there where the true loners sing freedom in war!*

And when the shadow of the fifth solitude disappeared, the "sixth" one came and started talking to me like this: *I am the shadow of your self; kill me if you want to be alone without witnesses. The seventh solitude is waiting for you. She will tell you the extreme secret. She will unravel the riddle of the ultimate mystery for you.*

...

The "seventh" solitude talked to me. But what she said to me remains one of my secrets. Who gives me the words to tell the mysteries of my deepest, innermost realities?

Who would understand me?

Oh my solitary, unknown brothers, don't you hear, in your darkest depths, the roar of a "No" without arguments? Well, this is my "No," my brothers.

8

A long series of macabre visions passes before my eyes.

They are the baleful and monstrous phantoms of my old faith.

They have bloodstained mouths and grip the dead in their bloody teeth.

The dead who fell whispering "tomorrow! ..."

The first dead one said: *I burned and robbed in the name of God, and I died for his glory, killing.*

The second one said: *I burned and robbed in the name of my fatherland, and I died for its grandeur, killing.*

The third one said: *I burned and robbed for the good of the people, and I died for their freedom, killing.*

The fourth one said: *I burned and robbed for the good of humanity, and I died for the love of it, killing.*

The fifth one said: *My mind was filled with a great sublime ideal. I dreamed that all human beings were free, great, and happy. I wanted freedom and equality, love and brotherhood to take possession of life and dominion of the world. And to realize this dream—which the world didn't want to understand—I robbed and burned and died, killing.*

And behind the corpses of these five murderous slaves, five portions of the world stand divided, ready to slit each other's throats while traveling down the same road.

...

God, fatherland, society, people, humanity? Ideal future?

But I am a reality, and I live today!

Is war the reality of life? Indeed! But I am not a sacrificial animal. I don't want my spirit to be a slave; I don't want my body to be sacrificed on any altar; I don't want any monster to crush my bones. You still cry out your anathemas,

whether priests of the people, servants of the fatherland or apostles of humanity.

You still cry out your calls for crucifixion against me. You cry out against the savage egoist, but I am not moved. I sing my iconoclastic songs of negation and revolt. I sing my noontime poem.

—The dog-day poem of my hot summer!

9

For me, Anarchy is a means for achieving the realization of the individual, and not the other way around. Otherwise, Anarchy would also be a phantom.

If the weak dream of Anarchy as a social goal, the strong practice Anarchy as a means for individual realization. The weak created society, and society gives birth to the spirit of the law. But the one who practices Anarchy is the enemy of the law and lives against society. And this war is inevitable and eternal. It is inevitable and eternal, because when the Czar falls, Lenin rises; when the royal guard is abolished, the red guard comes... Anarchism has been, is, and always will be the ethical and spiritual heritage of a tiny aristocratic horde, and not of masses or peoples. Anarchism is the exclusive treasure and property of the few who hear the cry of a "No" without arguments echoing in their most subterranean depths!

10

I belong to the most extreme breed of intellectual vagabonds, to the "cursed" breed of restless ones who cannot be assimilated. I love nothing that is known, and even friends are the unknown ones.

I am a true atheist of solitude, a loner without witnesses!

And I am singing! I am singing my songs woven from shadow and mystery...

I am singing for my unknown brothers and for my distant children...

I have freed myself from the slavery of love to feel free in my hatred and contempt...

Because I don't feel with the mind of the crowd. I don't suffer the pain of the people. I don't believe in a possible social harmony.

I feel with my own mind, suffer my own terrible pains, believe only in myself, in my own deep sorrow. This sorrow that no one understands and that I love, that I love through hatred and contempt for the human lie. Because I love this sorrow of mine. I love it as I love everything that is my own. Like my ideal lovers, like my unknown brothers, like my distant children.

11

So where are the ones—the geniuses or maniacs—who know how to live and die, alone and liberated, shouting— consciously and knowingly: "I" "Today" "My freedom" "My realization"?

Oh, my brothers, where are you?

Oh, "cursed" breed, when will your deep "humanity" be understood? But then, does all this need to be understood?

Doesn't the purest beauty still live ignored?

12

How terrible is my tragedy, how strange and deep my mystery.

I still dream!

I dream of friends never known, lovers never possessed, ideas never created, thoughts never thought, men never experienced, flowers never smelled, forests never hiked, oases never discovered, suns never seen... I dream!

I dream a great, tremendous revolt of all those who have grown pale in the long wait. I dream of the satanic awakening of those who live in chains... It must be beautiful to light pyres in the night!... To see death's centaurs running through every land ridden and spurred on by tragic heroes who've grown pale in the long wait. To see the spirit of revolt and negation dancing supreme over the world!...

Alas! I am still the eternal dreamer I always was!...

And yet the voice of reality tells me: The Czar dead, Lenin rises... The royal guard abolished, the red guard comes...

Yes I am a dreamer of the impossible, but I practice Anarchy, I don't dream it. I have condemned today's humanity, and I stretch the bow of my will to realize myself against it—not within it. For now I quench my thirst only at the spring of my inner beauty.

Oh, my unknown and solitary brothers, what will there be for our distant children?

And yet there must be future for evil too, because the hottest noon has not yet been discovered for man.

If today our "fate" damns us to live against the world, why couldn't their "fate" tomorrow choose them to dance freely over the earth? "Tomorrow!" But today?

All that is left for us today is to howl the tragic No of our negation and revolt.

Through the realization of our individuality; through the conquest of our freedom; through the full and total possession of our lives! Because we—vagabonds—are the individuals of revolt and negation who cannot be assimilated!

Il Proletario, vol.1, no.3, Pontremoli, August 15

Whip

Mr. Sectarian from Lodi,

I read in #13 of *Iconoclasta!* the vulgar and shit-filled[23] content that you—under the title "Individualism or Futurism?"—wanted to congratulate yourself on vomiting against me.

Here it is: I knew that you were an epileptic socialistoid from the time when I still had the Franciscan patience to read your scientific(?), philosophical(???) miscarriages thoroughly worm-ridden with putrid petty morality.

I've noticed that you were an impotent, sectarian, Jesuit slaverer from the time that I—with the calm and certain superiority that characterizes me—sat down again with a friendly and ultra calm writing (a writing in which I even stroked your vanity to induce you to accept a discussion) in response to that bilious and stupid attack you addressed to me. A response before which you ran away like a coward, no longer even finding—due to your prideful impotence—the strength to confess your polemical inability to support what you had erroneously thought! That you believed yourself (usual default) a lesser eternal father of anarchy without having understood even its ABCs is a fact that by now even children must know: even some supportive readers have noticed that you are a hysterical persimmon jealous of my pen—and have blushed with shame for you.

That your mind is a lurid mix of bigotted and priestly Manzonian[24] morality saturated with anti-anarchist and antilibertarian christian intolerance is a thing which, if I'm not mistaken, you still have to be made aware of yourself: that you are a blind and

---

23   I am taking some liberties here. The adjective Novatore used in Italian is *"stercorario,"* which translates into English as "stercory," a word that refers to a sheltered place for holding dung. I figured it was best to translate Novatore's intent in the clearest possible way in English.

24   That is, "in the style of Alessandro Manzoni." Manzoni was an Italian poet and novelist who promoted religious and patriotic values in his works.

fanatical worshipper of the ministerial reactions and anti-anarchist philosophy of that equivocating ape-like creature of thought and art that answers to the name of Benedetto Croce[25] is a logical consequence of your inferior mentality as a clumsy elephant of volitional thought and a crystallized mummy of intellectuality.

That you try to reinforce your theses(???) with the aid of a certain Mr. Max Nordau who all the perfect idiots celebrate as "Great" because he was one of the greatest slanderers of genius and of art is another logical consequence of your stunted inability to understand the heights and depths of the most refined and rarest minds. That you have found a place in anarchism, this is also—due to the near incapacity of anarchists to be able to make distinctions—a natural thing. But what is not natural, nor anarchist, nor human is that idiotic cynicism of yours that you dared to aim at me. You, forgetting that you have that old account of gold and sun to settle with me, open another one with me of dung and mud. Certainly, senseless cynicism is inconceivable for me. You call my writings— that you, with your inferior, four-eyed, pedantic moralist's mentality, could never understand—"literary (?) ravings" (how that utterly stupid question mark set there in parentheses demonstrates your unhappy rage!) "empty and insane prose," etc., etc.

And after comparing me (oh, how your depth renders you a soothsayer...) to dazed, alcoholic decadents ravaged by opium and weakened by the sirens (you wouldn't by chance, Camillo, also be a EUNUCH physically along with being one spiritually?) you're also pleased to classify me as a "graphomaniac" and a "megalomaniac."

I instead—to balance well my accounts with you—classify you as a COPROMANIAC. A classification, this one, that I will

25   An early 20th century Italian idealist philosopher and occasional politician who contributed to the theories of classical liberalism and who at first supported the Italian fascist regime, though he later turned against it. He was the minister of public education for a year in Italy and then moved on to the Senate there in 1910.

give with no fear of having to lie.

●

I almost have the firm conviction of having treated you as you deserved and of having satisfied you beyond any words.

You were looking for a fine, strong, and virile male, healthy in body and mind, who knew well how to handle the challenge of flogging your limp, wilted, senile mentality a bit, and you have found him.

Be ever so grateful for it to your Max Nordau and to government minister Benedetto Croce, your inspirer and teach of morality. As for me, I am an ANARCHIST, which means: an AMORALIST.

Your morality disgusts me.

And now, before making point, I make it my duty to let you know that I no longer have any time or patience to lose with you. This time I wanted to be indulgent and give you the publicity that you yearn for so much. But enough now!

To your hysterical, sectarian dribbling, only the high and solemn note of my scornful silence will respond. The worse for you if, not recognizing your conceited presumption, you go on believing that you're a professor of science and anarchism.

Therefore, take care: you want to purge anarchism of "loonies." But fools, beyond being poor wretches, almost always move one to compassion.

And you—know it well—are among these!

Iconoclasta!, vol.I, no.1–2, February 20

1923

In Defense of Heroic and Expropriating Anarchism

Crime is the vigorous manifestation of the full, complete, exuberant life that wants to freely expand itself and rejoice beyond every rule and boundary, not recognizing obstacles either in persons or in things... And it is precisely this, the aesthetic side of crime, that redeems it, exalts it, and raises it into the clear and sparkling light of a genuine work of art.
—T. Brunetti

The black news of the Torinese newspapers of last September 26 had to and wanted to concern itself with the capture of five of our best known comrades who fell into the slimy clutches of the police while—according to "precise information" that reached the same—went out in a "very elegant car" well armed with bombs, Brownings, and magnificent machine gun-pistols to carry out a ... "job" of two hundred and more thousand *lire*!

This is, in a short summary, the substantial content of all the long, endless columns of rude and vulgar prose pompously embroidered of cop-like tall tales published by the Torinese newspapers of last September 26, about the daring failed "job."

The comment—our comment—on the event in Torino taken in itself is this: "The Torinese police were themselves the ones who organized the 'job' through a sinister agent provocateur—the chauffeur who drove the 'incriminated' car—with the goals of glory, career, and cash."

And our comment is based on facts and evidence. Facts and evidence that, furthermore, cannot be missed by any of those who, reading the news of that day, saw in what way the "daring" (sic!) capture of the five anarchists happened...

2

Aside from the fact that the five comrades of ours who fell into the vile and infamous trap set for them by the police are really victims of the Judas chauffeur who betrayed them and sold them out, among the five there was also the beautiful and virile figure of De Luisi, romantic and passionate character of the rebel and hero, whose life is all a poem of daring battles and conscious rebellion, which perhaps very few anarchists have been able to write factually in the book of the life they lived.

Comrade De Luisi Giuseppe was—after all the bitterness, disappointments, and struggles experienced in the midst of the crowds—a terrorist and an expropriator. And today it is of him that I intend to speak here. Of him and the expropriating principle of heroic anarchism.

Many comrades will not approve of us, many others will not understand us, it's quite true, but from our point of view this is not a sufficient reason to persuade us to silence our iconoclastic voice, to break off our unbridled cry, to chain the wrists of our rebel thought.

We are neither madmen nor idiots, but we are anarchists and anarchists of a good sort.

3

Some people—many, too many people who act as *militants*—this inappropriate and anti-anarchist word—in our milieu and who enjoy the privilege—a poor and sad privilege—of being considered by most—most, even in our milieu, alas! are unfortunately a herd—as the sole, unique, true guardians of the divine fire that burns and sparks on the mystic altar of the sacred Vestal Virgin, of Saint Anarchy—have already been barking for a long time, for much too long a time, that the dark era of heroic anarchism is now fortunately surpassed, that the time has finally come to no longer let ourselves be dominated by the dark and tragic shadow of Henry and Ravachol, that Jules Bonnot's rebel automobile was only a sad and tragic expression of anarchist decadence condensed in a certain intellectual degeneration of bourgeois morality; that theft is not and cannot be an anarchist act, but rather one derived from bourgeois morality itself; that ...

But what's the use of going on? Let's stop here!

4

There are three reasons, for us, that serve to defend the terroristic act and individual expropriation.

The first is of a social, emotional, and human order and embraces theft as a *necessity* for material conservation of that individual to whom, though having all the predispositions of the sacrificial animal ready for any sacrifice and any commitment, society equally denies the most miserable means for an even more miserable existence.

For this individual, who the sadistic and lewd society is amused—through the macabre games of its bestial perversity—to confine ultimately to the last stages of human degradation, Enrico Malatesta himself—who cannot be accused of having a pagan, dionysian, Nietzschean concept of anarchism—allows that theft, besides being a right, may also be a duty.

But truthfully, to allow this kind of theft, it seems to me that there wouldn't even be an absolute need to be anarchists.

Victor Hugo, Zola, Dostoyevski, Gorky, Turgenev, Korolenko, and a whole long royal court of romantic and realist, humanist and neo-christian artists and poets have allowed, explained, and justified this kind of theft around which they have even created genuine masterpieces of art and beauty in whose pages the most lyrical of all human pity throbs and vibrates.

And it isn't just artists, poets, and novelists who explain and justify it, but the famous jurist, Cesare Beccaria himself, after having recognized that *laws, in the present state, are only the hateful privileges which sanction the tribute of all to the rule of the few,* affirms that *theft is not a crime innate to man, but rather the expression of poverty and desperation, the crime of that most unhappy portion of human beings to whom the right of property has granted nothing but a cruel existence.*

Over this first reason for theft there is therefore no need—we believe—to linger long, demonstrating what now no longer needs to be demonstrated.

We can simply add that for the man to whom society denies bread, if there is a *crime*, it is precisely that of not stealing, or not being able to steal.

I know, there are unfortunately still malignant derelicts with a human semblance, who exalt and praise the "great" **virtue** of the "honest poor."

They were—Oscar Wilde says—the ones who deal by their personal account with the enemy, selling their rights as first-born for the vilest plate of bad lentils.

To be poor—and "honest poor"—means, for us, to be enemies—and the most repugnant enemies—of every form of human dignity and every higher feeling.

What can an "honest poor man" symbolize, if not the most degrading form of human degeneration?

5

War is another thing. I am by nature warlike. To attack is among my instincts. So said Friedrich Nietzsche, the strong and sublime bard of the will and of heroic beauty.

And the second anarchist reason that serves to defend the

terroristic, expropriating act is a heroic reason.

It is a heroic reason that embraces theft as a weapon of power and liberation that can be taken up only by that daring minority of exuberant ones who, while belonging to the class of discredited "proletarians," have a vigorous and lively nature, rich in free spiritedness and independence, who cannot accept being chained in the shackles of any slavery, whether moral, or human, or social, or intellectual, and so much the less, economic slavery, which is the most degrading, most mortifying, most shameful slavery, impossible to bear when healthy, leonine, and throbbing blood pulses through the veins; when the tragic flashing of a thousand impetuous storms thunders in the mind; when the unquenchable fire of endless renewal crackles in the spirit; when the shadows of a thousand unknown worlds sparkle in the imagination; when the quivering wings of a thousand unsatisfied yearnings beat in the flesh and in the heart; when the heroic thought that burns and destroys all human lies and social conventions flashes in the brain.

And these tiny, exuberant, and daring minorities, dionysian and apollonian by nature, now satanic and now godlike, always aristocratic and unassimilable, scornful and antisocial, are the ones who, invaded by the anarchic flame, form the great perennial bonfires where every form of slavery is burnt up and dies.

And these mysterious and enigmatic, but always anarchic, natures were the ones who, willingly or unwillingly,

wrote with letters of blood and fire, passion and love, the glorious and triumphant hymn of revolt and disobedience that breaks rules and laws, moralities and forms, pushing crude and heavy humanity forward along the dark path of the centuries, toward free human life together, which perhaps these anarchist heroes no longer believe in; they were always the blazing torches that cast the phophorescent light of a new life into the dark social shadow; they were always the great heralds of the revolutionary storms disrupting every social system in which every free, uncastrated individuality felt itself odiously suffocating.

6

If anarchist philosophy—which proclaims the autocracy of the individual over the oligarchy of phantoms—has its phosphorescent roots embedded in the casing of the deepest, most mysterious human feeling and quenches its thirst at the immortal springs of human thought, it still has its green, luxuriant foliage up in the heights, in the glory of the sun where it sings, amidst the contrasting uproars of the winds, the tragic beauty of its heroic and reckless protagonists who have their feet in the guts and their brain in the sun of the idea.

And this is why, aside from the two reasons mentioned, a third reason of a higher order serves to defend heroic and expropriating anarchism: an aesthetic reason!

In fact, the "anarchist of the deed" is such a marvelously suggestive and terribly fascinating figure, whose mysterious, complicated, and deep psychology has been of use to not a few geniuses of tragic art as godlike and creative material for heroic poems overflowing with healthy immortal beauty.

And since there is not incompatibility between crime and intellectuality—Oscar Wilde says—it is logical that "anarchist crime" cannot and must not be looked upon by anyone as anything but a crime of a higher order.—Material and property of tragic art.—Not "black news" to satisfy the greedy and monstrous appetites of the crude and bestial, fatally corrupted herd.

7

If I have committed a crime—Wolfgang Goethe cried— *that crime would no longer deserve this name.* And Corrado Brando in *More*

Than Love says: *If this of mine is a crime, let all the virtue of the world bow down before my crime.*

And like the German poet and D'Annunzio's hero, so the anarchist cries. Because the anarchist is a vigorous child of life who redeems crime, exalting—with this—his Mother.

8

What does it matter if today, yesterday, and tomorrow, morality—this malign and dominating Circe—labels, labeled, and will label as "sin," "sacrilege," "crime," and "madness," the heroic manifestation of the daring rebel who decided to rise above every crystallized social order and every preestablished boundary, who wants to affirm—through his own might—the unbridled freedom of his I, in order to sing—through the tragic beauty of the deed—the full, anarchist greatness of all his individuality fully liberated from every dogmatic phantom and from every false social and human convention created by a most deceptive and repugnant morality before which only fear and ignorance bow?

Good and *Evil* as they are valorized by the vulgar herd, and interpreted by the people and by the rulers of the people, are empty—if still frightening—phantoms against which we turn, with full and mature consciousness, all our sacrilegious irreverence made up of Stirnerian logic along with the roaring, superior, serene laughter of the wise man Zarathustra.

On the tablets of new human values we are writing with our blood—which is the volcanic blood of dionysian and innovative antichrists—an other *good* and an other *evil.*

Who doesn't know it?

We are like the wind of the high mountains when it comes out from the mysterious chaos of its deep caverns to fertilize the virgin light of the dawn with the barbarous, furious, and roaring embrace of its vigorous and stormy nature, to later annihilate itself in the

231

titanic effort of creation and disperse itself into the infinite.

And the Joy and Sorrow that come from this fertile, creative embrace celebrated with iconoclastic ritual in the sacrilegious temple of the broadest freedom are the Good and Evil on which is raised the triumphal arch of our supreme anarchy, synthesis of Stength and Reality, Beauty and Dream.

Life, for us, is a wild flower that has to be cultivated on the frightening edge of immeasurable abysses.

9

In the hellenistically tragic soul of our comrade De Luisi Giuseppe, all three anarchist reasons—the ethical, the heroic, the aesthetic—named above had to stormily wander about there, condensed together forming a single and unique sparkling element that made of him—child of the night—a Demon-god of audacity and will, enthusiasm and might. The enchanting God of Ryner's wise parables who shouts: "I love you and want you, oh my *necessity*!" must have spoken to him in the silence of this deep and fearful night in which his soul found itself suspended between a dawn and a dusk, between a death watch and a mass of redemption.

That night in which—hounded, disappointed, starving—he retreated into himself for a solemn revision of his way of feeling and operating.

He saw the masses that he loved, and that he wanted to redeem with his blood, passing before his sight as a long line of cowardly and vile sheep that never rise up and that when they rise up, they rise up only find a new master before which to be able to bow their heads. And while one voice rose from the depth of his spirit howling: *Futility!*, another voice still more powerful rose from the guts of his darkest instinct, wildly called him back to the joy of intense living.

And he obeyed this last voice and, digging a grave in the

evening to bury the corpse of his dead illusions, he rose in the new dawn with all the violence of an implacable challenge.

And it was Him. He was a whirl... A Sign! A cloud heavy with storm—a lightning bolt that illuminated the path!...

His new life was like a mountain wind when it comes out from the mysterious chaos of its deep caverns to fertilize the virgin light of the dawn, with the furious and roaring embrace of his vigorous and stormy nature, to annihilate himself in the titanic effort of creation and then calmly disperse himself in the infinite...

And it is from the creative effort, celebrated with iconoclastic ritual in the sacrilegious temple of the broadest and truest *freedom* by these superb Heroes of Unbelief, that the new *Good* and *Evil* flows, like steaming blood, that we are writing on the bronze tablets of new human values.

And it is on the granite boulders of these new values that arises the glorious and triumphant phosphorescent arch of our instinctive Anarchy, tragic synthesis of Strength and Reality, Beauty and Dream!

10

"He, De Luisi Giuseppe"—says the black news of the Torinese newspaper of last September 26—"was not one of the usual robbers from the outskirts who, ragged and barefoot, confront the first passerby, pillage him of a hundred lire, go to a filthy dive in the company of the first prostitute that ends up in their arms to quickly help them consume the miserable fruit of armed robbery and to later denounce them to the police who in their turn rush to take them out of circulation and confine them in jail. No, De Luisi was a new Bonnot, perhaps more clever, who organized colossal robberies in the very center of the biggest cities and then withdrew in the guise of an unknown to live his life, laughing to himself at the vain police searches that actively sought him for a robbery of several hundred thousand lire that a state employee went through several years ago, as well as a revolt, gun in hand, in a Torino bar against police agents, many of whom were left seriously wounded, while a comrade of De Luisi— Milesi—was killed by the police in this same battle."

And here it is necessary, for once, to render our sincere homage to the hired press which—with obvious intentions of depicting De Luisi with the menacing colors of the dangerous criminal, have managed to give us an almost exact profile of the daring rebel.

Yes, De Luisi—who several years ago was still guilty of being an (honest) railroad worker who organized his coworkers, teaching them the word of liberation, when—for this "offence"—society first threw him in prison and then denied him work and threw him to its margins as insane rubbish, at which point he accepted the glove of challenge and on the margins became a hero!

A hero with a heart full of strength and love, a hero who was able to bear hunger and all privations rather than lowering his dignity to small and easy prey, a hero who was always able to give his solidarity—with passion—to comrades less daring or less fortunate than him; a hero who, with a hundred like him, would have devastated a regime. He loved danger like a brother and had in his soul the force of a thousand audacities.

And now that a vile Judas Iscariot has sold him to the black police of Turin and has had him buried—perhaps forever—in the darkness of a cell without him at least being able—for the last time—to sell his freedom at a dear price, we have the duty not to forget him.

It is necessary to rip off, once and for all, the lying mask that too many of us still keep glued to the face and recognize in him one of our best. No more of the rude comedy of our solidarity only with the "innocent." If the innocent deserve it, there are some of the "guilty" who deserve it even more than the innocent!

"Guilty" should be for us synonymous with *Best*.

And one of the best, among us, was precisely De Luisi.

His life in the last several years is a heroic poem and only art could tell its beauty and sing the great—if still dark—epic....

You who live on the fringes, remember him! You have lost in Him one of your best brothers: one of those who pointed out—through the example of action—the paths of that radical and deep rebellion that is peculiar to anarchist negators.

L'Adunata dei Refrattari, vol.I, no.22, New York, July 7

posthumous

Eternity's Song
fragments unpublished in Novatore's lifetime

Here is the vast, tranquil sea, my calm and peaceful sea!
  Small boats already flank the smiling cliffs.
  How frail and elegant the small boats are!
  Oh my pale and melancholy friends with titanic, heroic hearts, come, come! My hour has come and found me at peace. Already the fishermen with beautiful silver hair have arrived on the sun-drenched sands of the beach. Don't you see the golden oars there as they shine in the sun? Don't you see that up there in the distance, the bride is smiling down at us?
  Here I sit, waiting for you!

•

So have you arrived?
  I have never seen a sky as serene as your faces, my friends! How beautiful it is to understand each other and to depart together, unarmed, on such a long journey...

•

Everything is ready! Honey and sweet drinks for our children and fresh roses for the immaculate face of out bride. Let's go then, oh friends, Eternity awaits our roses!
  How could we die yet again after we have celebrated our wedding with Eternity and prepared the sweetest drinks for our immortal children?

•

We are alone, alone. I am on a small boat lost at sea. There is no more dawn, or dusk, or destination! In the depths, in the heights, and where they meet, we have only sun. Light, heat, greatness, depth and distance! What do you think, friends? Aren't you happy, then? Don't you see all this magnificent, endless space?
  And the roses, where are the roses?
  Don't you feel Eternity's highest kiss brushing your forehead?

Don't you hear her demanding the bride's crown?

•

Oh! What a poor, what a miserable thing was that arid land where we once lived! Do you still remember it, my friends?

Down there the sun rose and night fell! Down there men measured time. Oh! friends, friends! I am assailed by an infinite pity for that poor land! No... let's forget.

•

How many thousands of years will it be, my friends, that we float on the waves of these vast depths which rise up to the regions of the sun; up above the sun? And how many thousands of years will we yet live?

Oh! jolly Eternity, endless, happy now!

Friendship and Friends

A "Man" said to me: *I don't understand your ideas, and I don't approve of your way of thinking; but I don't believe you're absurd.* Without answering him I dodged him and continued my stroll on the opposite sidewalk.

Why? Simply: because I discovered yet again that the time has not come when a friend can say to his neighbor: *Your ideas and your thoughts don't interest me; but I admire and appreciate the mysterious whole of your individuality.* When a man will be able to pronounce this and other words with the lively voice of sincerity to express his thought transparently, without veils, the path that will lead him into the realm of friendship and love will be marked out.

Our time is made of camouflaged hatred and of a low and insidious war: all words of Love and Friendship are scented veils but hide the poisoned steel that brings nothing but pain and tears.

That "I don't believe you're absurd" of the man who spoke to me showed, with all vividness, what hid behind his apparent benevolence. Therefore, I left the individual without a response and dodged him.

I believe that when it's not possible to rely on the friendship of a being, the least that one can do is declare oneself his enemy.

I sincerely appreciate those who refuse the affectionate gestures of my heart. They are worthy of my sword. I should be clear: I possess a heart and a sword, and enjoy being as generous with the one as with the other.

One day a "Friend" said to me: *What you write and say matters only relatively to me, however I am very interested in appreciating what you feel. And I believe that words will be lacking in expressing your emotions... and so you will find the way that no one understands you.*

Therefore, don't speak, and allow me to look into your eyes where I will read your innermost being, and I will try to guess your state of mind!

I lowered my eyelids until it wasn't possible to penetrate into the depth of my transparent pupils, so that he couldn't probe into the depths of my mind. I know, from experience, the dangers of guessing. In the secrecy of my brain I think that possibly that day ended with losing a "Friend."

Today, when I wandered in search of some missing wreck of my size, I found... a friend.

But, can I believe that this friendship will be an enduring thing?

Such a question isn't frequent in me, and it's most difficult to give it an answer. I come to think almost with certainty that while I probe into my suppositions, he remains calm, and shortly he will no longer be my friend. Friendship is such a tenuous, such a garish thing, such a weak thing, that I find it almost justified that certain individuals give up looking for it. Will they cry out at the title *misanthrope*? No! In every instance they are loners!

I am one of them, because I hate human beings who make a law of living in community, while I appreciate those who know how to remain alone.

The feeling of solitude is the most elevated of human emotions. It belongs at the same time to strength and to beauty.

Besides, loners are the ones who have spread the most benefits over humanity.

And for this "grateful" Humanity despises them.

In summary: the loner chooses few friends, because hypocrisy and lying repulse him.

Ruta, Paris, 1950

Renzo Novatore
by Enzo Martucci[26]

My soul is a sacrilegious temple in which the bells of sin and crime, voluptuous and perverse, loudly ring out revolt and despair.

These words written in 1920, give us a glimpse of the promethean being of Renzo Novatore.

Novatore was a poet of the free life. Intolerant of every chain and limitation, he wanted to follow every impulse that rose within him. He wanted to understand everything and experience all sensations—those which lead to the abyss and those which lead to the stars. And then at death to melt into nothingness, having lived intensely and heroically so as to reach his full power as a complete man.

The son of a poor farmer from Arcola, Italy, Abile Riziero Ferrari (Renzo Novatore) soon showed his great sensibility and rebelliousness. When his father wanted him to plow the fields he would flee, stealing fruit and chickens to sell so that he could buy books to read under a tree in the forest. In this way he educated himself and quickly developed a taste for non-conformist writers. In these he found reasons for his instinctive aversion to oppression and restriction, to the principles and institutions that reduce men to obedience and renunciation.

As a young man he joined the Arcola group of anarchocommunists, but he was not satisfied with the harmony and limited freedom of the new society they awaited so eagerly. "I am with you in destroying the tyranny of existing society," he said, "but when you have done this and begun to build anew, then I will oppose and go beyond you."

Until he was fifteen years old, Renzo included the church in his poetry. After that, freed and unprejudiced, he never planted

---

26   Translation by Stephen Marletta, revised.

any roots in the gregarious existence of his village, but often found himself in conflict with both men and the law. He scandalized his respectable family, who wondered what they had done to deserve such a devil...

...Novatore, who was influenced by Baudelaire and Nietzsche, asserted that we had needs and aspirations that could not be satisfied without injury to the needs and aspirations of others. Therefore we must either renounce them and become slaves, or satisfy them and come into conflict with Society, whatever kind it may be, even if it calls itself anarchist. Novatore:

Anarchy is not a social form, but a method of individuation. No society will concede to me more than a limited freedom and a well being that it grants to each of its members. But I am not content with this and want more. I want all that I have the power to conquer. Every society seeks to confine me to the august limits of the permitted and the prohibited. But I do not acknowledge these limits, for nothing is forbidden and all is permitted to those who have the force and the valor.

Consequently, anarchy, which is the natural liberty of the individual freed from the odious yoke of spiritual and material rulers, is not the construction of a new and suffocating society. It is a decisive fight against all societies—christian, democratic, socialist, communist, etc, etc. Anarchism is the eternal struggle of a small minority of aristocratic outsiders against all societies that follow one another on the stage of history.

Those were the ideas expressed by Novatore in *Il Libertario* of La Spezia, *L'Iconoclasta* of Pistoia, and other anarchist journals. And these were the ideas that then influenced me as I was well-prepared to receive them.

During World War I Novatore refused to fight for a cause that was not his own and took to the mountains. Astute, courageous, vigilant, his pistol at the ready, the authorities failed at every attempt to capture him. At the end of the war the deserters were amnestied and he was able to return to his village where his wife and son were waiting for him.

I was sixteen years old and had run away from home and my studies, freeing myself from my bourgeois family,

who had done everything they could to stop my anarchist activities. Passing through Saranza on my way to Milan, I stopped to get to know Novatore, having read his article

"My Iconoclastic Individualism". Renzo came at once to meet me together with another anarchist called Lucherini.

We passed unforgettable hours together. Our discussions were long and he helped me fill gaps in my thinking, setting me on my way to the solution of many fundamental problems. I was struck by his enthusiasm.

His appearance was impressive. Of medium height he was athletic in build, and had a large forehead. His eyes were vivacious and expressed sensibility, intelligence and force. He had an ironic smile that revealed the contempt of a superior spirit for men and the world. He was thirty-one years old, but already had the aura of genius.

After two months wandering around Italy with the police at my heels, I returned to Arcola to see Renzo again. But Emma, his wife, told me that he was also hunted and that I could only meet him at night in the forest.

Once again we had long discussions and I was able to appreciate his exceptional qualities as a poet, philosopher, and man of action even more. I valued the power of his intellect and his fine sensitivity which was like that of a Greek god or a divine beast. We parted for the last time at dawn.

Both of us were existing under terrible conditions. We were in open struggle against Society, which would have liked to throw us in jail. Renzo had been attacked in his house at Fresonaro by a band of armed fascists who intended to kill him, but he had driven them off with home-made grenades.

After that he had to keep a safe distance from the village.

Despite being an outlaw, he continued to develop his individualist anarchist ideas in libertarian papers. I did the same and we aroused the anger of the theoreticians of anarcho-communism. One of them, Professor Camillo Berneri, described us in the October, 1920 issue of *L'Iconoclasta* as *Paranoid megalomaniacs, exalters of a mad philosophy and decadent literature, feeble imitators of the artists of opium and hashish, sirens at so much an hour.*

I could not reply because in the meantime I had been arrested and shut up in a House of Correction. But Renzo replied for both of us and took "this bookworm in whom it is difficult to find the spirit and fire of a true anarchist" to task.

More than a year later I was provisionally released from prison, but I could find out nothing regarding the whereabouts of Renzo. Finally I received the terrible news that he had been killed.

He was at an inn in Bolzaneto, near Genova, along with the intrepid illegalist S.P., when a group of *carabinieri* arrived disguised as hunters. Novatore and S.P. immediately opened fire and the police responded. The tragic result was two dead, Renzo and Marasciallo Lempano of the *carabinieri,* and one policeman wounded. This was in 1922: a few months before the fascist march on Rome.

So a great and original poet, who, putting his thoughts and feelings into action, attacked the mangy herd of sheep and shepherds, died at the age of thirty three. He showed that life can be lived in *intensity,* not in *duration* as the cowardly mass want and practice.

After his death it was discovered that, together with a few others, he was preparing to strike at society and tear from it that which it denies the individual. And in the Assizes Court where his accomplices were tried, a prosecuting counsel acknowledged his bravery and called him *a strange blend of light and darkness, love and anarchy, the sublime and the criminal.*

A few friends collected some of his writings and posthumously published them in two volumes: *Above the Arch* (*Al Disopra dell'Arco*) and *Toward the Creative Nothing* (*Verso il Nullo Creatore*). Other writings remained with his family or were lost.

So an exceptional man lived and died—the man I felt was closest to me in his ideals and aspirations. He described himself as "an atheist of solitude" He wanted to "ravish the impossible" and embraced life like an ardent lover. He was a lofty conqueror of immortality and power, who wanted to bring all to the maximum splendor of beauty.

ABOUT RENZO NOVATORE

by Renzo Ferrari, his oldest son

> *...True freedom is a privilege of despots who dominate*
> *and great rebels who don't know how to obey.*
> *But both are beyond law and rule,*
> *both are beyond mediocrity.*
> —Renzo Novatore

Renzo was not a "pacifist", but it was precisely because he intensely loved "war" that he hated it intensely. And for having given his lordly "NO!" to this (1915-1918) he was condemned to death. But here he is still in 1920, recalling his dangerous fugitive years:

... and if the green forest clasped a BANDIT in its flowery arms, the stinking barracks and the loathsome trenches didn't shut the soldier in their muddy mouths.

But when at times I passed through the endless, green prairies and—in spring—looked upon the whole marvelous feast of flowers that stretched out like a scented, laughing lover along the silent banks of a solitary river, I wasn't able to conceive why other men could search for me with such mindless and brutal stubbornness to bring me death. Why—I asked myself—shouldn't a bouquet of these fresh and wild roses be enough to disarm the mindless rage of these ones who want to kill me? Why before so much music, so much poetry, and so much beauty shouldn't everyone born of woman fraternally embrace his like, moved?

And under this tragic and desperate nightmare my young head bowed, moved, gloomy, and pensive, seeking—but in vain—a precise answer to this eternal Why?

And then my rebel and vagabond thought galloped dizzyingly toward the desolate biblical forests where human brotherhood had its origins in Cain and Abel, and I bitterly thought that five fifths of humanity was nothing other than an obscene remnant of barbarity, an ensemble of mud and cowardice, hypocrisy and deception whose sublimation has been and will always be impossible. And as I heard the murderous cannon echo from the Trentino cliffs, I thought that, from Cain on, only the strongest is right.

These thoughts, which could scandalize all the "conventional thinkers," all the "moral snivelers," all the nauseating hypocritical "humanists," are nonetheless the feeling of a deeply sincere Man who is not afraid to look straight in the face of reality, and confront it. Of a Man who, without hiding behind any cover finally proclaims the "Lordship of himself" and boldly, in Art as in Life, goes beyond the rusty gates of "Good" and "Evil" and encounters Death.

...

excerpted from "A proposito delle 'Quattro Difese'"
("About the 'Four Defenses'")
Il Corriere della Spezia, July 25, 1954

STANDARD FREETHOUGHT WORKS